W9-BQX-185

Family-Friendly Communication for Early Childhood Programs

Deborah Diffily and Kathy Morrison, editors

National Association for the
Education of Young Children
Washington, D.C.

Second printing November 1997

National Association for the Education of Young Children
1509 16th Street, NW
Washington, DC 20036-1426
800-424-22460 or 202-232-8777
Website: http://www.naeyc.org/naeyc

The National Association for the Education of Young Children (NAEYC) attempts through its publications program to provide a forum for discussion of major issues and ideas in our field. We hope to provoke thought and promote professional growth. The views expressed or implied are not necessarily those of the Association. NAEYC wishes to thank the editors and contributors, who donated much time and effort to develop this book as a contribution to our profession.

Library of Congress Catalog Number: 96-71080
ISBN: 0-935989-78-1
NAEYC #330

Editor: Carol Copple; *Design and production:* Sandi Collins, Jack Zibulsky, and Angela S. Dixon; *Copyeditor:* Sandi Collins; *Editorial assistance:* Anika Trahan and Penny Atkins.

Printed in the United States of America

About the Editors

Deborah Diffily is an assistant professor of early childhood education at Texas Wesleyan University. Before teaching at the college level, she worked for eight years with young children and their families as a kindergarten and first-grade teacher. Deborah serves on the boards of the Texas and the Fort Worth Area AEYCs—two NAEYC Affiliate Groups.

Kathy Morrison is an assistant professor of child development at Tarrant County Junior College in Fort Worth, Texas. As a High/Scope-endorsed trainer in the Preschool and K–3 Approaches, she has served as a consultant in many locales. She is coauthor of a book for kindergarten teachers, *Beginning Science*. Kathy has served on the boards of the Texas and the Fort Worth Area AEYCs—two NAEYC Affiliate Groups.

Contents

*The editors and the NAEYC publications staff collaborated in the writing of this article.

Math and Science

Social-Emotional Development

Family Matters

*The editors and the NAEYC publications staff collaborated in the writing of this article.

Preface

This book grew out of our own struggles as early childhood educators trying to share with parents our knowledge and educational approach. Over the years we found ourselves constantly looking for ways to help parents understand what we mean by developmentally appropriate practice, to communicate the importance and value of play, and to gain parents' support. When Kathy was the director of a child care center on a community college campus, she wrote monthly newsletters to parents and included short articles about pertinent early childhood issues as often as she could. She used excerpts from resources such as *A Parent's Guide to Early Childhood Education* (Dodge & Phinney 1990). She pulled quotes from *Developmentally Appropriate Practice* (Bredekamp 1987) and attempted to explain what DAP principles mean in the classroom. But coming up with descriptions and explanations of practice that speak to parents is never easy and takes time, a valuable commodity in our lives.

Realizing that other directors must be having the same problem, Kathy, along with Paula Weaver Blackshear, designed a workshop to address this need. At the 1990 NAEYC Annual Conference, they presented "ADAPting Parents: Helping Parents Understand Developmentally Appropriate Practice," a workshop which included theory, samples of the parent pieces they had written or collected from other directors, and opportunities for the participants to practice writing their own pieces. The workshop was very well received; several participants suggested that a book of such articles would come in handy. Kathy and another colleague, Cathy McFerrin, presented the workshop twice at the High/Scope Registry conference in Ypsilanti, Michigan, with the same encouraging results. Hence, the idea for this book was born.

When the two of us—Kathy and Deborah—went in 1993 to the NAEYC Leadership Conference in Washington, D.C., we saw that a book of this kind would make a wonderful Affiliate project. We talked about asking fellow members of the Fort Worth Area AEYC to contribute short articles on good early childhood practice. We would serve as editors to put together the volume. The book could be sold to raise funds for our Affiliate.

The Fort Worth Area AEYC Executive Board brainstormed the "hottest" topics and parent concerns and then sent out a request to Affiliate members for contributions. The members responded quickly and professionally, and Bob Haffner applied his computer wizardry to format the book. In September 1995 we published the first version of this book. Sales were brisk at the Texas AEYC State Conference in Dallas. Heartened, we approached NAEYC to see if the book might be published nationally.

We gratefully acknowledge the contributing members of the Fort Worth Area AEYC for their time and effort in helping make this book a reality. The individual names of the contributors are listed in the table of contents. Each author has made a significant contribution to the field of early childhood education.

We are particularly grateful to Carol Copple and Sandi Collins for their patience in coaching us as editors and for the many hours they dedicated to *Family-Friendly Communication* to make it into the book it is.

—*Kathy Morrison and Deborah Diffily*

Each of the 93 articles in this book conveys useful information and key understandings on a topic of interest to families. In addition, we have suggested other opportunities and strategies for communication with families. The book's purpose is broader than providing articles and activities on specific topics. We sought to create a book that will inspire early childhood educators to develop and nurture a deeper, richer level of communication with families, to build mutual trust, and to help parents understand the many ways that they can contribute to their children's development.

It is our hope that having these articles handy to use as a starting point will help busy teachers and directors to maintain the regular, informative communication with families that we all know is vital. And whether we like it or not, families' lives (not to mention our own!) have become more hectic and tightly scheduled. With this pressure on adults for their time and energy comes an increase in the importance of written communication with families. Often parents find out what is going on in the program not by a leisurely chat with the teacher on the playground but by going through the child's backpack at night or reading a weekly newsletter. Gathering families together for occasional meetings is invaluable—there's no substitute for the "up close and personal"—but with parents' work schedules and the demands on their time, we can't count on frequent, well-attended family meetings for realizing all our communication goals.

No one can put more hours in the day for staff or parents, but in this book we provide practical tools that will give you a head start as you strive to communicate with today's busy families.

The volume contains several elements that you will find useful in your communication with families. A few points need to be made about each.

Elements of the book

1. Articles for parents

These boxed messages, numbered 1 through 93, are designed to be easily photocopied for inclusion in a newsletter, as a handout, or in a packet of materials. You do not have to request permission to copy or adapt the material; we created this book to make these articles available for ready use. At the same time, keep in mind that you will increase the value and impact of these messages to parents if you take time to tailor the "generic" article to your own program—more on that later.

To help you find other articles relating to the subject at hand, cross-referenced articles are listed by article number in the "See also" box at the bottom of each page. We include these to make it easier for you to look over the various articles pertinent to the topic you want to address. These numbers will be handy when you are trying to decide which article is best suited to your current need, when you are considering using several (in combination or in a series), or when you want to look at other activities or strategies relating to a given topic or concern, as described in item number 3 on the next page.

2. Tips for adapting and using the article

On many pages of this volume you will see material adjacent to the box. Italicized text above the line relates to adaptation or use of the article. With one article we might suggest including children's drawings or comments; in another instance, we might stress ways that an article needs to be adapted to the families in the program.

Tips for adapting and
using the article

Articles for
parents

Other
strategies for
communicating
with families

Other
articles
relating to
the subject

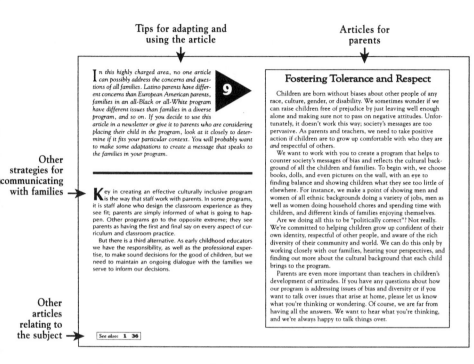

3. Other strategies for communicating with families

Below the line in the material adjacent to the box, you often will find suggestions for extending or reinforcing the main ideas of the article. We offer far more suggestions than you would ever use in a year. And, no doubt, you already have a set of activities and strategies that you like to use with parents. The ideas in this book will get you thinking of new things to try.

4. Resources

Beginning on page 113 is a listing of annotated resources, divided into those primarily for parents and those intended for staff.

Making a message your own

Your messages to parents will be far more effective if they are more personal, specific to *your* program and the children in it. When you have found an article in this book that seems helpful for communicating with parents on your chosen topic, take it as the starting point and adapt it to your program. You'll increase the impact tenfold. Here are some ways to tailor and personalize the articles.

- In an article that describes children's activities, you can add the names of children in your class or program (see next page). If the newsletter goes to parents from different classes in your center, you'll need to identify each child's group or teacher. Take care, of course, not to leave any child out. A good way to make sure everyone gets equal time is to keep a list, checking off names as you use them.

- Mention specific books, activities, and games the children enjoy and those they have been involved with recently.

- Include anecdotes or recent events that have happened at school or that parents or children have related ("Brian and his dad found a box turtle the other night at the park. They went to the library and read about what turtles like to eat."). These can be written into the article or used as sidebars or highlights.

- Include children's artwork or samples of their writing.

- Try using black-and-white photographs, if your method for reproducing the newsletter permits. Good photographs often photocopy surprisingly well, and they can also be used for classroom displays.

- Alert families about upcoming activities and describe projects that are going on or have recently been completed (see example on next page).

These examples show some of the things you can do to make messages your own.

*   *   *

You will think of other ways to adapt these articles and make use of them. For instance, when parents visit the program to determine if they want to enroll their child, the director can give them several articles to communicate key aspects of the program's philosophy. Among the many benefits of informing parents—those already in your program and those who aren't—about the whats and whys of early childhood education is that they become advocates for high-quality, developmentally appropriate programs—and they appreciate having their children in such a good program.

The articles here are also useful for staff development, particularly for new staff who do not have much preparation in child development. If you are a director, you may want to give a new staff member several core articles to read as an introduction to the philosophy and practices of the program. A few days later you can talk with the staff member to provide clarification on any points the newcomer doesn't understand and to discuss with her the classroom implications.

Veteran staff, as you know, may need to be reminded of the reasons for what they do in the classroom, since we all too easily begin to do things on "automatic pilot." When teachers

---

Wonderful , Wet Water

Diane, Jimmy, and Su Lee are at the water table, pouring water back and forth between two containers. **Diane** watches as the water overflows and runs down the side of one container. **Jimmy** feels the cool liquid against **his** skin and listens to the sounds of the water as it moves. **Su Lee** observes the containers that float and those that sink, and she tries to get one of the heavier containers to float. **The children** are exploring, discovering, and testing objects in the water.

Adaptation of #18

Fingerplays and Action Songs

Rhymes and movements for the hands and fingers, some of which date back almost 2,000 years, are still used in early childhood classrooms, as well as the more modern action songs that involve the whole body.

Fingerplays and action songs are a fun way to learn. They are a great way to pass a few minutes of transition time—while you are waiting in the car, in line at the grocery store, before or after dinner.

Children love repeating familiar rhymes, so come back to the same songs enough so that your child remembers the words of the rhyme and the movements that accompany the words.

Perhaps you remember a fingerplay from your childhood that you can share with us. If you do not know fingerplays or action songs that are appropriate

for your child's age just ask us—we'll be happy to share the fingerplays we do with the children.

Last week, when Ms. Rita introduced a new song about our bodies, she stopped when she got to a word that began with *h*. "What do you think that word might be?" she asked the children. "Head!" shouted several kids.

"How did you know that? "Ms. Rita asked. "We saw the *h*," explained Ali, "and we knew the word rhymed with the 'bed' from the line before. And the song was about parts of us. So it must be 'head.'"

As you can see, the children already are attending to context and letter sounds when they are trying to identify words they see in print—terrific strategies for developing reading skill!

Addition to #38

---

are going through their paces mechanically, they are not as effective as they could be and are sure to be missing opportunities to foster children's development and learning. Nor are they ready to explain to parents what is going on in the classroom and why. To help staff revisit and refine their understanding of a certain aspect of developmentally appropriate practice, you can copy one or more of the articles to give to teachers as a basis for discussion in staff development.

Early Childhood Fundamentals

The following articles are grouped together because they reflect early childhood educators' basic beliefs about the way young children develop and learn. Each addresses one or more aspects of developmentally appropriate practice for children ages 3–5.

The articles are designed to help parents understand the basic philosophy of the program. Parents know their children well, but many families need and want to know more about what educational experiences benefit children's development.

When parents enroll their child in your program, you need to emphasize that you believe in children actively learning through real materials and that your program reflects this belief. It is always a good idea to take the parents through the center, pointing out what the children are doing in each area of the classroom and describing the learning that is going on.

A packet containing a few of these articles can then be given to the family to read at a later time. This will help reinforce what they have seen and heard when they were at the center.

1

What Is "Developmentally Appropriate Practice"?

You probably have noticed that our classroom has a lot of bustle and noise, that children are up doing things, talking, playing, and exploring. Such a classroom environment differs from the old grade-school images of a teacher doing a lot of talking at a blackboard while children sit and listen quietly at their desks.

Research and experience tell us that to be effective with young children, teaching practices need to be "developmentally appropriate." What this means is simply that educators need to think first about what young children are like and then create an environment and experiences that are in tune with children's characteristics.

Early childhood, after all, is a time of life quite different from adulthood, and even from the later school years. Children 3–6 learn far better through direct interactive experiences than through just listening to someone talk. They learn extraordinary amounts through play and exploration. And the younger children are, the more what they learn needs to be relevant and interesting on the day they learn it, not just in the context of some future learning.

Based on such knowledge about what children of this age are like, we design our program to fit them. It works a lot better than trying to redesign children!

A developmentally appropriate program like ours is age-appropriate. But that's not all. To make the program a good place for every child, we gear our classroom environment and activities to this community and the families involved. We're eager to learn as much as we can about each child's family, cultural background, past experience, and current circumstances. With this knowledge we work to create a program that fits the children and the families we serve.

The Power of Play

Have you ever heard someone remark about an early childhood program—even ours, perhaps—"All the children do there is play"? At good early childhood programs there *is* a lot of play—and there should be!

Years of research on children's learning and development document the many benefits of play for children's intellectual, social, emotional, physical, and language development. Children at play are actively involved in creating themes, exploring and establishing environments, solving problems, and developing shared understandings.

Children play in many ways. They play independently, sometimes near each other but with each child engrossed in his own activity. They engage in what is called "parallel play," perhaps using each others' toys or even talking, but not coordinating their play. They also play cooperatively, organizing roles and scenarios for group play. As they get older, children are capable of more cooperative, coordinated play. But all kinds of play are valuable.

As kids play with each other, they learn to see other children's points of view and begin to become more empathetic and caring. They come to understand customs and rules in their own culture and to appreciate those of others. They learn to use language in new ways to describe their play and to interact with others. And in play, children develop their muscles and coordination.

Adults support children's play by providing space, opportunity, and materials. We set up areas where kids can play without fear of damaging furniture or injuring themselves. We make sure that they have the time to choose and to become engaged in their own play activities. And when we provide them with simple, interesting materials—no newfangled, expensive gadgets required—kids take it from there.

Play is fun. But it also is serious business that pays big dividends to its eager, young investors.

Parents sometimes ask us, "All they do is play?" or "Will they be ready for kindergarten or first grade?" This article can help answer those questions. But what else can we do?

A family meeting can be a valuable tool. Below is a sample outline for a meeting that focuses on the value of play and children's active involvement.

1. Welcome the families and explain that the evening will be devoted to communicating the philosophy of the program and the value of play.

2. Divide participants into two groups.

3. Have one group go to a table that has bubble-making liquid, all kinds of wands, rubber bands, paper cups, and so on. Tell the group members that they can play with the bubbles and explore the materials in any way they choose. One teacher stays with this group to assist, to extend, and to enhance their play.

4. The second group is to sit in a circle. One large jar of bubbles and a single wand are provided. Parents are to take turns using the wand to blow bubbles. Only two blows are allowed, and the wand and jar then pass to the next person. The other parents are to sit quietly and watch as the materials are used and passed on. One teacher stays with this group, making sure that they follow the rules exactly.

5. After a few minutes of bubble exploration in each group, stop the activities. Ask the parents to go back to their seats. Lead a discussion on the differences in the two

(continued)

See also: **1** **3–4**

(continued from p. 4)

activities. Write on chart paper what was learned in the passive activity and what was learned in the active activity.

For the passive activity you might get responses such as
- We learned to take turns.
- We learned to wait.
- We learned to follow rules.

For the active activity you might get responses such as
- Bubbles are wet and sticky.
- You can use a lot of things to make bubbles.
- Whatever the wand shape, bubbles are always round.

6. Ask the parents about the focus of this activity. They probably will respond with something about learning about bubbles. Ask which group learned more about bubbles. Which group enjoyed the experience more?

7. Summarize the experience. *Active learning is messy, sometimes noisy, and usually fun. And much more learning is achieved when there is an opportunity to explore materials.*

8. Then discuss how active learning is the basis for the program. Explain the emphasis on helping children become problem solvers and active investigators.

9. Finally, give families an opportunity to ask questions. They may want to know what, if anything, teachers do to extend children's experiences beyond the active "messing around" just experienced. Share with them some of the things you would do to make the most of the bubble activity.

The Best Learning Is Active Learning

Active learning takes advantage of children's natural desire to move and touch. Young children love to manipulate items and explore new ideas. They enjoy the opportunity to see how things work and to test their own theories.

Active learning takes advantage of children's natural motivations, abilities, and interests. Kids get lots of opportunities to investigate what interests them—to solve problems, discover relationships, and make comparisons.

Children use all their senses to make discoveries: *how heavy is it? does it smell? can I find another one that feels the same? what does it sound like when I drop it? how is it different from the other items?* Using their hands, eyes, nose, ears, and mouth to explore an item, children gather more information and remember what they learn.

As they interact directly with the environment, children not only gather sensory information, they also refine their senses and motor skills. For example, it takes very refined movement of the hands and fingers to produce the penmanship required for writing. Squeezing clay, picking up puzzle pieces, and lacing threads through beads are ways for young children to practice using hands and fingers.

We organize the classroom environment to promote active learning, and we do lots of things to encourage children to think and talk about their discoveries and creations. The next time you want your child to learn about something, provide the materials, space, and time. Then step back and watch. You will be surprised at how much more the child will discover through active involvement.

Dynamic Classrooms
Are Not Quiet!

Quiet classrooms do not mean that young children are learning. In fact, since oral language is very important during the early years, quiet classrooms may indicate that young children are *not* learning all they could be.

Talking gives a child the opportunity to experiment with new words. It provides the vehicle for expressing ideas and testing current knowledge.

Shared experiences are important; they give children something to talk about. Children learn the nuances of communication in groups by trying out their language skills. For example, they learn what a question sounds like and how loud is loud enough.

Using words and talking about how things work, making comparisons, and retelling experiences lead to increased intellectual development. When children reconstruct experiences, sequence events, and point out similarities or differences, they are clearly engaging in higher-level thinking skills. And when kids are encouraged to ask questions, they not only gain information from adults' responses but also build their competence—and confidence—as active seekers of knowledge and understanding.

The vocabularies children use in reading and writing are based on the words they are familiar with from listening and speaking. But expanded vocabularies and other aspects of language growth occur through using language. Talking in the classroom may be a little noisy, but positive results are easily heard!

See also: **2–3 5**

Parents are naturally drawn to photographs of their own children. You can effectively share information about developmentally appropriate practice by displaying photographs of children engaged in a variety of learning activities.

Take pictures of children as they explore materials, build with blocks, paint or draw, work with playdough, read books, and engage in other activities. And, of course, make sure that each child appears at least once in the display.

You might title the display "What Am I Learning?" Under each picture you can list the things the child learns through the particular kind of play. Here's an example.

When I paint at the easel, I am

- developing imagination and creativity;
- practicing eye-hand coordination, helpful for learning to write;
- learning the names of colors and how to make new colors;
- learning to distinguish shapes and create shapes;
- noticing patterns, which is useful in science, mathematics, and music; and
- forming concepts of symmetry, balance, and design.

Letting Children Choose

Why do we as adults pursue hobbies such as golf, crochet, or gardening? We spend time in such an activity because we find it enjoyable, we have some control over the activity, and we see it as offering some probability of success. We choose what we will crochet or plant; we decide where, when, and with whom we will play golf or tennis.

Children, too, learn best when they have some control over their learning, when activities are meaningful and relevant, and when they can make choices in the materials they will work with and how they will use them.

Children thrive when they have opportunities every day to make choices in their learning. We facilitate children's choices within a carefully planned environment. We create the environment to allow each child to choose activities that are developmentally appropriate for his or her age. The children choose the peers with whom they will work and play and usually determine how they will use the available materials.

These choices empower children to take control of their own learning. Children use materials and equipment in far more creative and innovative ways than we could ever plan, and they use the materials in ways that meet their own developmental needs.

Research indicates that intrinsic motivation—when we work on a task primarily because we find it satisfying—is the most effective and engaging way to learn. In this program we make an effort to provide materials and activities that provide choice and interest for the children. That's a key reason that you'll see busy, involved children when you visit the classroom.

Process and Product

As adults, we are concerned with the outcomes or the product of our efforts. We want the report to look nice, the cookies to taste great, or the hedges to be perfectly straight. We participate in few activities just for the fun of doing them.

In part this is because we are not still learning how to do most of these activities. But do you remember when you learned how to play tennis or golf? Or use a new computer program? In the beginning you needed to do a certain amount of "messing around"—exploring what would happen if you did this or that.

That is the way it is with your child. Kids are learning new things all the time, and they need the freedom to try things out without worrying about the product.

Luckily, young children tend to be more involved with the process or the doing than they are with the end product or results. That is why your child may draw all afternoon yet still not be able to tell you what he drew. And why one child can pour rice back and forth between pitchers all day long, and another will string and unstring beads every day for a week.

It is hard for us adults to look beyond the product of an activity and see what the child is learning from the process. Perhaps he's learning coordination or beginning writing skills or making discoveries about triangles or gravity. He's certainly finding out that doing for one's self is very satisfying—and that builds confidence.

Be patient. Allow your child the time to grow and learn through the various processes that are part of the task. Enjoy watching his or her involvement. Later, we all can be proud of the product.

When a family member dropping off or picking up a child pauses to examine a painting or other creation, take this opportunity to point out what went on during the process of the child's work. An end product often does not reflect the intense effort the child put into it or the child's feelings about her work.

For example, point out that "Meg worked 20 minutes on creating that ocean with dots of blue paint." Or "Billy and Sue experimented with several bridges before they constructed that one." Or "Charlie enjoyed mixing those colors. He kept pointing out how they changed as he added white or black."

In case you don't have the opportunity or time to speak with an individual parent, jot down your comments on a sticky note and put it on the back or corner of the picture for parents to see. Or leave a brief message on the family's answering machine or voice mail.

See also: **2 5 30 42 59**

Some programs have integrated Howard Gardner's contributions on multiple intelligences; others have not. If you haven't read Gardner's theory and applied it in your program, don't use the piece until you have done so. Parents find the topic intriguing and immediately begin asking which intelligence their child has and what you are doing about it in the program. It's best to wait until you have a grasp of multiple intelligences before introducing the idea to parents.

Staff and interested parents can get acquainted with Gardner's fascinating and important work through accessible resources such as Thomas Armstrong's *Seven Kinds of Smart: Identifying and Developing Your Many Intelligences* (Penguin 1993). It includes games and software that are attuned to each of the intelligences.

More Than One Kind of Smart

"He has a low IQ."

"She's very intelligent."

Sometimes we talk as though intelligence were a single commodity that people have in greater or lesser supply. Yet we see all around us adults and children who are very smart in math but not at all good with words, musically gifted but klutzy on the athletic field, and so on. Most of us, in fact, struggle with some tasks and sail through others.

Educators now know more about this variety in individuals' "intelligences"—the modes we use to interact with the world—thanks to the work of psychologist Howard Gardner. Seven of these intelligences are described by Gardner.

Children with a **musical** intelligence have a natural ear for melody, rhythm, and other musical elements; **spatially oriented** children enjoy reading maps and exploring how mechanical devices work. Other children are more at home using their **linguistic** aptitude—telling stories, playing with words, and reciting tongue twisters. Strong **logical-mathematical** intelligence shows up not only in math aptitude but in enjoyment of games and problems requiring logic and reasoning. Children who learn best when they are moving and handling things rely on their **bodily-kinesthetic** intelligence. An affinity for the natural world and its creatures stands out in children with a **naturalistic** mode of intelligence. Finally, children who make friends easily and have plenty of "street smarts" are **interpersonal** naturals, while quiet thinkers and strong-willed debaters shine in the more internal, reflective **intrapersonal** mode.

All of us have preferred modes of intellectual functioning. At the same time, we need to use each of the modes in one situation or another. Recognizing the various ways that children think and learn, teachers can help children both to use their individual strengths and to become more adept in learning modes that are *not* their strong point.

Asking Open-Ended Questions

A question like "What color is that block?" evokes a one-word answer. But an open-ended question, "Tell me about the blocks you are using," encourages a child to describe the blocks or explain what she is doing. There is no right or wrong answer here.

An answer to an open-ended question gives us a window into what the child is thinking and feeling. And the response is sometimes wonderfully creative. In explaining or describing, children also use language more fully.

In our program, we try to think of good questions to ask children. You might hear one of us say to a child,

- Tell me about your picture.
- What else can you do with the playdough?
- What could you use to make the tower stand up?
- What do you think would happen if ——?
- Is there another way to ——?

It is difficult to change the closed-end question habit. But when we ask open-ended questions, children reap great benefits as they think through their responses to express what they want to say. And with their answers, we find out more about what they think and feel.

Parents are better able to ask open-ended questions that spark the child's response (as opposed to the lead-balloon what-did-you-do-today variety) when they have specific information about upcoming events. For example: Learning from the newsletter or monthly events calendar about some special activities in the 4-year-olds' classroom, a parent can ask, "What did you like most about Mr. Insect Guy's visit today?" Or, "Tell me about the insects that you saw."

It makes little difference whether the event information is provided through computer-generated calenders, narrative letters, or newsletter articles/lists. What is important is keeping families informed of the day-to-day activities of the program.

To fill in parents on something special their child did that day, send a note in the backpack or leave a brief message on the family's answering machine.

See also: **62 76**

In this highly charged area, no one article can possibly address the concerns and questions of all families. Latino parents have different concerns than European American parents, families in an all-Black or all-White program have different issues than families in a diverse program, and so on. If you decide to use this article in a newsletter or give it to parents who are considering placing their child in the program, look at it closely to determine if it fits your particular context. You will probably want to make some adaptations to create a message that speaks to the families in your program.

Key in creating an effective culturally inclusive program is the way that staff work with parents. In some programs, it is staff alone who design the classroom experience as they see fit; parents are simply informed of what is going to happen. Other programs go to the opposite extreme; they see parents as having the first and final say on every aspect of curriculum and classroom practice.

But there is a third alternative. As early childhood educators we have the responsibility, as well as the professional expertise, to make sound decisions for the good of children, but we need to maintain an ongoing dialogue with the families we serve to inform our decisions.

Frances Kendell (1996) describes three things that we as teachers or directors can do to increase the chances of creating a culturally inclusive environment that staff *and* parents support: build strong relationships with families; continue the ongoing process of examining our own biases and attitudes; and create strategies for involving parents and addressing concerns about what to include in the curriculum.

Fostering Tolerance and Respect

Children are born without biases about other people of any race, culture, gender, or disability. We sometimes wonder if we can raise children free of prejudice by just leaving well enough alone and making sure not to pass on negative attitudes. Unfortunately, it doesn't work this way; society's messages are too pervasive. As parents and teachers, we need to take positive action if children are to grow up comfortable with who they are *and* respectful of others.

We want to work with you to create a program that helps to counter society's messages of bias and reflects the cultural background of all the children and families. To begin with, we choose books, dolls, and even pictures on the wall, with an eye to finding balance and showing children what they see too little of elsewhere. For instance, we make a point of showing men and women of all ethnic backgrounds doing a variety of jobs, men as well as women doing household chores and spending time with children, and different kinds of families enjoying themselves.

Are we doing all this to be "politically correct"? Not really. We're committed to helping children grow up confident of their own identity, respectful of other people, and aware of the rich diversity of their community and world. We can do this only by working closely with our families, hearing your perspectives, and finding out more about the cultural background that each child brings to the program.

Parents are even more important than teachers in children's development of attitudes. If you have any questions about how our program is addressing issues of bias and diversity or if you want to talk over issues that arise at home, please let us know what you're thinking or wondering. Of course, we are far from having all the answers. We want to hear what you're thinking, and we're always happy to talk things over.

Around the Early Childhood Classroom

Early childhood teachers plan the classroom environment and schedule to include a range of activities that contribute to children's development, such as dramatic play, art, construction, music and movement, sand and water play, and experiences with oral and written language. The articles in this section give parents a brief description of each activity and what it does for children. (The next section, *Learning Together at Home and School,* returns to some of the principal activities of early childhood classrooms but with greater emphasis on the connections between the program and home. Other key areas of the early childhood curriculum are the focus of sections *Toward Literacy* and *Math and Science.*)

13

10

During your first family meeting of the year, give parents a chance to explore the areas of the classroom. Children can help guide their parents through some of their favorite activities. For example, one child might take his family first to the block area, first explaining what he likes to do in this area and then inviting his parents to participate in the play. The child might then move to the art area. There he can show the materials that are available and do an open-ended art activity with his family.

At each area of the classroom there could be a large poster that outlines the skills that can be practiced and learned in this area. The teacher can point these out as she moves around to each of the areas.

Parents will begin to gain a firsthand understanding of all of the possibilities for learning in each of the areas. They also might note the hard work it requires to set up areas with appropriate activities and to facilitate the learning that takes place.

At the end of the exploration of the room's areas, adults and children can come back together to share some of their discoveries and to ask any questions they might have. Teachers can pass out handouts that outline what is learned in each area.

(continued)

Let's Pretend

Make-believe play is not only one of the great joys of childhood, it also offers abundant opportunities for children's development. Children develop interpersonal skills, particularly cooperation and conflict resolution, and improve their language and problem-solving abilities in pretend (dramatic) play.

Around the age of 2, children begin to pretend to cry, sleep, and eat. They soon include a stuffed animal, doll, or favorite toy in their play. They also begin to transform objects into symbols—a simple block becomes a fast race car or a stick makes a fine race horse.

As children approach 3, they begin participating in make-believe play with other kids. Dramatic play gradually becomes more elaborate and complex. Four- and 5-year-olds engage in socio-dramatic play, which provides opportunities to rehearse adult roles. Such play helps children make sense of the world.

These first dramatic experiences often focus on home experiences. Kids pretend to cook, clean, and care for younger children. That's why our dramatic play area has props and equipment that represent the home setting. These stimulate children to act out roles familiar to them.

Dramatic play fosters emotional development as children work through fears and worries in a safe context. Social skills are promoted as children communicate and negotiate their roles and actions. Another plus is that children use language more frequently and more elaborately in make-believe play than they do in virtually any other activity.

Parents can actively encourage dramatic play at home by capitalizing on their children's interest at the moment, developing themes from stories their children have heard or movies they have seen, and providing props for pretend play. Providing a home environment that is conducive to play stimulates intellectual and social development. At the same time, parents will be developing rich memories of their children at play—memories that last a lifetime.

The Artful Classroom

A child becomes totally engrossed, immersed in the process of making a work of art. The sensation of feeling the smooth thick paint sliding onto the easel paper calms the child and brings pleasure in the creation. When the child grapples with the challenge of representing an object or person on the page, she is engaging in a task that is both demanding and satisfying.

Teachers provide an assortment of art materials that children may choose from to make their own unique creations. We do not have the children copy a teacher's model or make a designated product. We encourage them to use the materials in different ways. Art is a vital and vibrant part of the early childhood program, contributing to all aspects of the young child's development.

As they draw, paint, and sculpt, children think creatively, make decisions, and solve problems. Children's fine motor skills are developed naturally through manipulation of brushes, crayons, scissors, and clay. All of these activities prepare children for writing in later years. Language also is developed as kids talk about color, shape, and size, and as they describe their work to friends and teachers.

To encourage your child's artistic enterprises, provide large blank paper (the ends of newsprint rolls can be purchased at a nominal cost from your local newspaper, or you can recycle paper by letting your child use the back of office paper), watercolors, markers, or chalk for use at home. Art supplies also make great gifts!

Value your child's efforts and expose him or her to quality artwork through visits to museums and art shows. Recognize that young children learn in a variety of ways and that creative activities provide positive, satisfying experiences for all children.

Including samples of children's artwork is a natural way to share their creativity with families. You can also put in specifics from your classroom to illustrate children thinking creatively, making decisions, talking about their pictures, and so on.

(continued from p. 15)

During parent conferences, family members again will ask questions about the program or need clarification on your philosophy and why you do things the way you do. You might take this opportunity to reiterate the value of the different activities and areas of the room and the learning that takes place in each of them.

Set up the conference room with a display on children's development and learning in the major curriculum domains and areas of the classroom. For example, the display might include photographs of children engaging in a range of activities. Under each picture could be a description of what the children are doing during this work time and what learning is taking place.

The parents can review the display, then sit down with you to examine a folder containing specific information about their child. This folder might include drawings, paintings, the child's dictation, and anecdotes of teacher observations of the child.

From this documentation and information that you share, families not only will be reassured that you know their child very well but also will gain a deeper understanding of your program and how it meets the needs of their child.

See also: **6 29–31 85**

12

Consider making use of the parent bulletin board to highlight various aspects of your program—art, blocks, dramatic play, writing, and so on. Post photos of children engaging in the featured activity, samples of children's work and what they said about it, and perhaps a description of the materials available in that area. You also may want to use the article from this book that describes the nature and value of children's engagement in the activity you are focusing on. Keeping the display up for at least a week will allow more parents to take a good look.

Learning with Blocks

Blocks are open-ended materials that stimulate young imaginations, provide choices for discovery and invention, and promote the development of problem-solving skills. One day a block may be an airplane. The next day that same block in the hands of the same child can be a sofa for the house he is building.

Building with blocks helps develop young children's eye-hand coordination, visual perception, and large and small motor skills. It builds self-confidence and provides opportunities for creativity and dramatic play. These things occur naturally when children play with blocks.

We also find that working with blocks often deepens children's engagement with literature and literacy. A child may be inspired, say, to construct the three bears' beds and chairs, a pirate boat, or an enchanted castle.

We sometimes take photographs of children's block creations and invite the children to caption the photos. We also encourage girls and boys to make their own signs for their creations. In these activities, children are exposed to print in meaningful ways.

Inviting children to reconstruct buildings and other things they have seen on field trips is one way we encourage their thinking in relation to social studies. They work with the concepts behind maps and models, and as they build block cities, farms, and factories, they work out their own understanding of these complex sites and communities. Children also develop mathematical and scientific concepts, such as balance and gravity, as they work with blocks.

Blocks are engrossing and fun for young children, of course. They are also invaluable tools for promoting children's development on many fronts.

The Reading Area

Our reading area is full of wonderful books that children love and learn from. We have a good collection ourselves, and we are always bringing in fresh books from the library.

Children have the opportunity to slowly leaf through good books that have been read to them, look at the pictures, examine the print on the page, and "read" to someone else. These experiences create a love of books that helps children become eager, and eventually proficient, readers.

The quiet, comfy atmosphere of the reading area gives children a pleasant place to escape from the noisy, vibrant classroom. This is a place for kids to rest, to have some time alone.

We continually look for quality books to add to our reading area. Let us know if you have any suggestions of books to add or if you would like to donate a book or help get good books from the library.

To instill a love of reading and to expand your child's vocabulary, read to your child at home! Be a partner with us in instilling a love of books in your children.

Parents often are very concerned about how the early childhood program is helping their child become a reader. The reading, writing, and listening centers of the classroom are very important in the development of good reading skills. You can help parents understand the value of these areas and see the learning that is taking place through exploration of the materials.

From time to time in the reading area, consider highlighting an author for a week or two. Post information about the author and books that he or she has written. Encourage parents to visit the library to check out books that are written by this author to read to their child at home.

Or focus on a genre. For example, have a good selection of folktale books for children to explore. Read one book each day and talk about how these stories have been passed down from parents to children. Ask parents to share folktales or fairy tales they remember from their youth. The children also could create and illustrate their own folktales.

See also: **30   39–40   44–54**

If you use this article in your newsletter or put it on the bulletin board, you may want to add a request for parents' help in gathering writing supplies. Many working parents will gladly share old stationery and envelopes, used computer paper, paper clips, canceled stamps, ink pads, and other materials.

Involving parents in providing materials for the center is a way to build a positive relationship with families. Parents get an opportunity to contribute to their child's classroom without having to spend time away from work.

Periodically send home samples of children's writing with a note describing what the child is working on and what writing skills he has already mastered.

Bring samples of the child's writing to each family conference. Showing samples of the child's growth and development in writing over the year—or from one year to the next—is a powerful way to communicate how much the child is learning in your program.

The Write Stuff

Long before a child learns to form letters with a pencil or marker, she has taken many steps toward learning to write. Children must have many opportunities to use their hands to do various things before they can successfully print letters.

Molding with clay, using large and small Legos, picking up beads, and playing with knobbed puzzles all prepare the fingers and hands for writing. Scribbling with markers and crayons, controlling a pencil for use with a stencil, using chalk on the sidewalk, and painting with fingers and large brushes are a few of the ways children practice for later writing.

We stock our room with plenty of paper, paper clips, staplers, pencils, markers, and crayons, and we make sure that these materials are available for children to use whenever they choose. Children may want to "write" notes to their friends or messages to their teacher or parents. They use writing materials in their dramatic play—making signs for a store, tickets for a show, menus for a restaurant, and so on.

As children experiment, developmental stages of writing become evident. Children move from random scribbling to controlled scribbles, to random alphabet letters, to consonants that represent words. Only with lots of opportunities to practice can children move through these stages.

If your child does not have a proper pencil grip, cannot purposefully manipulate a crayon, or simply shows no interest in learning to write, he or she probably is not ready to do so. Take care not to push. Children enjoy learning a new skill only when they are really ready for it. Getting ready is just as important as mastering the skill.

The Listening Center

Listening is the language ability that develops first and is used most often. True listening means not only hearing sounds in the environment but also taking meaning from and responding to those sounds.

Listening is an essential part of the development of both written and oral language. We can best help children develop listening abilities by providing experiences that encourage careful listening. Many of these experiences take place in our classroom listening center.

The listening center, a comfortable area where children can use a tape recorder, headsets, and a variety of audiotapes, gives them daily opportunities to listen to oral language and music. Through songs, poems, and stories, children identify and differentiate between familiar or similar sounds, rhyming words, letter sounds, and speech patterns.

Children's vocabulary, comprehension, and critical-thinking skills also get a boost. Listening experiences stimulate kids to express their own reactions in various ways, including verbal discussion, art, drama, or stories of their own. Through these activities children relate what they hear to their own experiences.

Families can extend this focus on "listening with a purpose" at home or during car trips. Try to identify particular sounds. Point out the differences in pieces of music. Play games with words by finding rhyming words or words that begin with the same sound. Don't make this a task—just have fun.

Sometimes parents assume that children just listen to stories at the listening center. A way to extend parents' understanding of the uses of the listening center is to list the numerous ways that the center is used.

Your newsletter article, handout, or bulletin board can give parents a better idea of the wide range of activities that go on in the listening area. For example, one program might give parents this description:

At the listening center

- We listen to audiotaped stories, including classics and folktales.
- We listen to nursery rhymes and other poetry with strong rhythms and sound patterns.
- We look at a book while we listen to the story on audiotape.
- We listen to classical music.
- We hear music from various cultures.
- We draw pictures while listening to a story or music.
- We play listening games, such as guessing environmental sounds.
- We do fingerplays that we have learned.
- We practice reading the book along with the tape of the story.

See also: **16   37–40   44   46**

With this article, issue a standing invitation for parents to share their musical talents and tastes with the children. Ask parents to bring their trumpet, violin, guitar, voice—whatever—to school and play for the children. Other parents could share favorite records or tapes, including those from different musical traditions. Used or blank tapes also can be donated by families.

After children develop their own dances and movements to different types of music or create a collection of their own homemade instruments, they could perform one or two songs or dances for other groups of children in the school. The band or troupe could perform during lunch hour or on the playground. Children also could perform on family nights.

If you can arrange it, allow families to check out audiotapes of the children's favorite songs. Add streamers, scarves, rhythm sticks, kazoos, and tambourines so that the children can share an evening of music and movement with their families.

The Sound of Music

Kids of all ages are naturally drawn to music. Infants coo at lullabies, toddlers bang on pots and pans with a wooden spoon, and preschoolers sing and dance to music.

Children learn a variety of skills from musical experiences. Shaking, tapping, and beating instruments enhance fine motor development. Children listening for a beat, the sounds of different instruments, tones, and lyrics are developing auditory discrimination.

Kids can experience the emotional effects of music by listening to and creating music that is soothing, exciting, or funny. Music promotes creative development as children experiment with new rhythms, sounds, and movements.

To encourage your child's exploration of music, you don't have to buy expensive instruments. You can make several simple instruments at home.

Kazoo—Let children decorate a toilet paper tube with construction paper and crayons. Help them put a square of wax paper over one end and secure with a rubber band. Blow through the open end while humming a tune.

Tambourine—Give the child two sturdy, luncheon-sized paper plates. Place a small quantity of dried beans or rice in one plate, then glue the plates together and allow to dry. The child can decorate with crayons, paints, and scraps of ribbon or other material. Shake the tambourine with one hand or tap it on the heel of the other hand.

Drum—Help the child cover the outside of a two-pound coffee can with heavy construction paper and decorate as desired. Replace the lid of the can and beat with hands or spoons.

Sand blocks—Sand two small pieces of scrap wood to prevent splinters. Help your child glue coarse-grit sandpaper onto one side of each block. Rub the blocks together to make noise.

Moving to Music

Young children are natural dancers. Even infants bounce up and down to the beat of music.

Enjoyable and natural as it is, creative movement helps children learn many concepts. It teaches them balance and coordination through challenging moves and postures. It teaches rhythm and beat as children choreograph their movements with music. It even promotes children's ability to predict what comes next by hearing repeated musical phrases. Creative movement is also an important tool for developing children's self-esteem and body awareness.

It's easy to engage children in dance and creative movement. Just move with them. Kids love dancing with their families. Turn on the radio or put on your old tapes or records and enjoy singing and dancing together.

Add to the experience by using movement props. Sheer or silky scarves are fun to use when dancing. These can be found at local thrift shops or dime stores. Streamers are also great fun for children. Just glue ribbon or paper streamers to short pieces of dowel rods. Rhythm sticks, used to keep time with the beat of the music, also can be made at home. Foot-long lengths of dowel rod can be sanded smooth and painted or left bare.

Try creative movement with your child. Play different kinds of music to expand the experience. This is a wonderful way to have fun together—and even to get some exercise!

See also: **16 22**

When using this piece in your newsletter or in another format, you might want to substitute the names of several children in your group for the fictional Dionika. And if you use this piece when the weather is warm, add a few ideas for playing at the beach, lake, or stream—or with the backyard garden hose.

18

The sand and water areas are probably the messiest areas of any preschool room and yet many times the most intriguing. While many parents hesitate to let their child make such a mess at home, the early childhood program is committed to supporting this kind of open-ended, creative, soothing play.

Because parents often don't realize the benefits of sand and water play, look for opportunities to draw them into the fun—whether at family meetings or during more informal times when families are in the classroom. (For water play, everyone needs to wash hands before starting.)

To help parents know what to do, provide some written guidelines or suggestions next to the sand and water table (see below). Then be available to help with questions or problems that arise.

Suggestions for parents

Begin by just following the child's play. Ask what she or he is doing. Let the child put into words the actions or plans. Follow your child's lead. Try not to direct the play. He or she will think of things to do with the sand and water that you do not.

Take turns. If your child pours one cup, you pour the next.

(continued)

Wonderful, Wet Water

Dionika is at the water table, pouring water back and forth between two containers. She watches as the water overflows and runs down the side of one jar. She feels the cool liquid against her skin and listens to the sounds of the water as it moves. She observes the containers that float and those that sink, and she tries to get one of the heavier tubs to float. Dionika is exploring, discovering, and testing objects in the water.

Children, and adults as well, are naturally drawn to water. Water is comforting and soothing. The feel and sounds are pleasing. The natural attraction makes the water table a perfect activity center for a preschool classroom.

Just think of all the learning that goes on! Children experiment with cause and effect, refine problem-solving skills, and learn basic math concepts such as volume, measuring, and comparing.

As your child takes a bath, encourage water play by adding different size containers to fill and empty or different household objects that will float or sink. Colanders and other objects with holes are sure to create some intriguing challenges. As your child and you explore the materials, talk about your discoveries together. Guide and extend the learning by asking questions such as "What would happen if ——?" "How does the water feel?" "Why do you think that happened?"

More opportunities for home water play include watering plants, adding water to the sandbox, blowing bubbles through a variety of frames, and freezing or melting water.

Sensational Sand

You've probably noticed—in your yard or at the playground—how much your child likes to dig in the sand. Sand is great fun, but it's also a wonderful material for learning.

Children learn mathematical and scientific concepts from playing at our sand table. For instance, when kids pour sand from measuring cup to measuring cup, they are likely to be learning about estimation, volume, texture, and even counting and simple physics.

As children play with sand, we encourage them to talk about what they are doing or experiencing. For instance, we might ask, "Does the sand feel different when it is wet?" or "How did you get the sand so smooth on your castle?"

Have you ever longed to dig your toes into the sand? Sand has the same soothing effect on children. We find that kids who are frustrated, annoyed, or angry often choose the sand center to work out those feelings.

You can encourage sand play at home by providing a sandbox. It does not need to be large. One excellent and inexpensive sandbox is a bin or busboy tray (available at restaurant suppliers and some discount stores and flea markets) filled with sand. Bins and trays are portable, easy to clean, and easily stored. Provide measuring cups and spoons and other plastic containers to support sand play.

Of course, spills and stray sand go with the territory. With indoor sand play, a sheet or large piece of plastic will help contain the mess, but the benefits are well worth any temporary inconvenience.

(continued from p. 23)

Ask questions such as
- What else can we do with that?
- Tell me about your ——.
- What can you add to make this better/different?
- How can you solve the problem with ——?

Parents who take the opportunity to sit for a few minutes and explore the materials will get a taste of the soothing nature of sand and water activities. They will see the total involvement of their child in sand and water play, as well as evidence of the thinking that such play provokes. When adults experience for themselves the pleasure and exploration that these fluid materials evoke, they begin to understand the intrinsic value of sand and water play.

This article can be changed to reflect your particular environment or climate. You can also tailor the text to the equipment and features of your outdoor area.

Parents appreciate specific suggestions about enjoyable outdoor environments to share with their children. Whether you live in a rural, urban, or suburban area, or in a desert, prairie, or coastal region, you will have outdoor environments that parents and children can share—and learn from.

In most regions the seasons also present changing opportunities for outdoor play. As the seasons change, suggest appropriate outdoor activities. In a colder climate or during winter, you might remind parents of the importance of daily outdoor play, despite the temperature, and of the advisability of wearing multiple layers of clothing.

Let's Go Outside!

Kids love to play outside! And teachers love outdoor time, too. It's a relaxing, stress-reducing, tension-relieving part of the day, and a time when much development and learning take place.

Physical development is evident outdoors as children learn about their bodies in space, practice important physical skills, and exercise and strengthen muscles. Children also learn social skills—cooperation, turn taking, being on a team. And kids learn about the world around them: they observe changes in plants and the differences in the seasons; they watch living things such as worms and crickets; they learn about the earth by collecting rocks and leaves.

The outdoor environment is an extension of the classroom. We plan for this part of the day just as we do for the other parts of the daily routine.

The environment includes equipment that helps encourage learning. For example, climbing equipment helps children develop their motor skills and judgment about what they can safely do; trikes and other riding toys develop balance and coordination; the sand area is used for creating cities and harbors and for exploring the properties of dry and wet sand.

We often bring classroom equipment outside to enrich the outdoor environment. One day you might see children painting at the easels and another day you might notice children bathing their babies and taking them for a ride in a wagon. The time spent outside is a valuable part of our daily schedule.

 See also: **22 62–64 87 89**

Growing with Group Games

Watch children at play and you'll see them creating their own group games as well as playing old standbys—enjoying the time spent together with other children. But the value of such games goes far beyond the fun kids have in playing them. Group games promote children's development in a variety of ways.

There are several types of group games: aiming games like Drop the Clothespin in the Bottle; races like Spoon Race; chasing games like Duck, Duck, Goose; hiding games like Button, Button; and guessing games like Charades.

In many games children develop their large motor skills as well as their eye-hand coordination. Children also develop many social-cognitive skills, from turn taking to negotiation, and they are challenged to see things from different perspectives.

In some group games children need to make comparisons and inferences and solve problems. Children who play games on a regular basis often begin adapting them or inventing their own games, which then adds another dimension to their learning and development.

These days many children have fewer opportunities than in the past to play group games in their neighborhoods. In our program we introduce new games, actively foster game playing, and enhance the developmental benefits through our conversations with children about their games.

See also: 26 87

22

To extend families' understanding of large motor development, get them involved in the play! Designate a "Let's Move Our Bodies" week and invite parents to take 15 minutes or so in the morning or at pickup time to explore the possibilities of the playground. Label each piece of playground equipment with the areas of the body that it helps to develop.

For example,

Climbing structure—upper body strength;

Swings—lower and upper body strength, coordination of body movement.

Besides encouraging parents to play with their children, this activity highlights the importance of physical development and how you promote it in your program.

Large Motor Development

Running, jumping, climbing, skipping, hopping, throwing, and balancing come naturally to young children, but kids need plenty of opportunities to practice them. These large motor activities are an important part of your child's day here. With daily large-motor experiences, children practice fundamental movement skills that help them develop good self-esteem and physical competence.

A developmentally appropriate movement curriculum facilitates basic movement skills and physical fitness, such as those named above. Children get the chance to run, jump, skip, walk on balance beams, and throw and kick balls. As with all skills, motor skills must be practiced to improve.

You might see us moving like snakes, cats, bears, dinosaurs, or frogs. Music gets us moving—we sometimes jog to release tension and we occasionally jump simply for the joy of it.

We want children to be physically fit because it's important to their health. But we also know they learn better when they are healthy and in good physical condition.

Fine Motor Development

To many people, fine motor development means the way a child holds and uses pencils, crayons, and scissors. But fine motor development is much more. To understand fine motor development it is important to understand a little about how the human body develops.

Human development progresses from the head down and from the trunk outward. The torso and shoulders develop long before the elbows, the hips long before the knees, and so on. In other words, skilled use of one's hands and fingers is the last in a long process of development.

Fine motor development is enhanced early in life by many opportunities to develop and refine large motor skills. It is developed by giving young children big pieces of paper and large crayons, allowing them to practice their movements. We also help children's fine motor development through a variety of activities, such as working with playdough, constructing with Legos and Tinkertoys, stringing beads, doing puzzles, and playing with pegboards and other table toys.

Such engrossing activities are better than tasks at which the child may "fail" or those that are very repetitive. Through these fun, natural activities, children improve their fine motor development without frustration or boredom.

A special day or week focusing on small motor development, similar to the large motor emphasis described in article no. 22, can help families see what children are learning to do in various classroom activities. On the tables, set art materials, playdough, Legos, or other construction materials, stringing beads, puzzles, and pegboards, and invite families to spend a few minutes playing when they arrive or before they go home. Through handouts or signs for parents, briefly describe how each of the materials enhances their child's fine motor skills.

This article sticks to rather general discussion because computer hardware and software vary so much from one classroom to another. Early childhood programs also use them differently. This parent communication will be more informative if you adapt it to your own computer resources and specifics, such as what programs the children are working with at the time, what the kids especially enjoy, and where they benefit from adult support.

Be aware that many parents cannot afford home computers or do not choose to buy them, yet they can see the value of giving children early experiences with computers. Find out what computer resources your community makes available for families—at libraries, community centers and the like—and share this information with parents through the newsletter, a special handout, or other means.

Computers and Young Children

In this age of technology, we recognize the value in introducing computers to young children. Computers in an early childhood classroom are another tool for kids to explore, to investigate, and to master.

We believe that computers are a valuable asset to our program, but only because our approach to computer use is geared to the way young children learn and develop. For example, we know that young children are developing social skills during these years, so we place the computer where children can interact as they work with it. At least two chairs are at the computer at all times. This arrangement allows for collaborative problem solving and sharing of ideas.

Children need to have opportunities to work independently of adults. The computer software that we use allows independent use. We choose software with verbal instructions or picture menus that allow children to work with little adult intervention.

Kids learn by doing. The software that we choose allows the child to explore concepts, determine the pace and the direction of the experience, and use their creativity. Developmentally appropriate software is open-ended and calls for thinking and active problem solving.

Just like blocks and paints, computers are a beneficial tool in an early childhood classroom. Children have the freedom to explore this tool in a supportive environment that encourages active exploration.

Learning Together at Home and School ▶

The articles and activities in this section help families understand what children learn through typical early childhood experiences. In each article we link the learning that goes on in the classroom environment to additional learning opportunities at home. Parents are given suggestions and ideas about activities they can do with their children. The articles easily can be extended by including simple recipes, patterns for puppets, and other how-to resources. Parents and teachers can work together to ensure a rich environment that stimulates children's cognitive, motor, and social development, both at home and at school.

If you've recently done some cooking in the classroom, incorporate into the article children's comments, parts of the process that children found particularly fascinating, or other anecdotes. When the food cooked together is a big hit with the children, you may want to print the recipe in the newsletter or in a handout.

Cooking is a terrific way to involve families in the life of the class. If the cooking activities are planned near noontime and parents are notified well in advance, many will be willing to use their lunch hour to take part. They can read recipes to small groups of children and help them follow the directions.

Of course, not all parents can take time away from work, but many can, if we just ask.

Cooking activities can be simple. Ideas include mixing margarine with green food coloring to cook green eggs and ham; melting cheese and adding chopped tomatoes for queso to eat with tortilla chips; dicing apples, celery, and pecans for waldorf salad; heating chicken broth and cooking rice for chicken soup; and boiling chopped vegetables in beef broth for vegetable soup.

Cooking also provides an opportunity for families to share foods that are distinctive to their cultures. Encourage parents to share simple, inexpensive recipes or snacks with the children.

Parents who see the excitement of children cooking at school are more likely to plan cooking experiences with their own children at home, so these shared experiences benefit children in multiple ways.

A Recipe for Learning

To children, the world of cooking is magical. We combine all kinds of ingredients, then stir, simmer, boil, or bake, and—presto!—something delicious is created.

Being asked to help with cooking makes kids feel grown up and important. And when they cooperate with others to make a dish, they take great satisfaction in producing something for everyone to eat.

Cooking with children—pointing out key words on the recipe as we go along, having them measure, pour, and stir—is a time of learning as well. Reading, science, and math concepts abound in cooking experiences. Children learn to recognize numbers and words from recipes. They begin to use vocabulary related to cooking. And they observe how ingredients change when they are mixed together.

Kids also learn basic math concepts such as counting, measurement, and part-whole relationships. It will take years before young children fully understand concepts like numbers, weights, measurement, time, and temperature, but repeated experiences with cooking promote the development of these concepts.

Cooking with young children does take more time than cooking alone. But the learning that accompanies cooking and the closeness fostered by the shared experience are worth the extra time.

Let the Games Begin!

Children learn best when activities are meaningful to them. Experts in the early development of mathematical concepts tell us that children develop mathematical understanding in situations in which number and quantity are relevant and important to them.

Games provide this opportunity. Playing games is a wonderful way for children to share time with family members, to have fun, and to learn. Kids love to play games with their favorite grown-ups.

In simple card games, such as Go Fish, Concentration, or Crazy Eights, children learn many different things. They identify numerals, match numerals or objects, and practice memory skills. They also develop fine motor skills by picking up and handling the cards.

By playing dominoes or games with dice, children learn to count the dots and to relate those dots to the number they represent. Moving game pieces the right number of spaces on a board adds the concept of one-to-one correspondence, and constantly comparing the rolled numbers helps develop number sense.

The games we choose should be appropriate for the age of the child. With commercial games, look for the age recommendations on the game box. Remember, noncompetitive games are best—young children hate to lose.

As we play games with children, we can extend their mathematical thinking by asking simple questions: *How many matches did you get? Do you have more red cards or more black ones? Would you like to deal us 6 cards each?* Continued opportunities to play games and talk and think about number concepts help children develop their own math understandings.

Because of the vast developmental differences in children within the age range of 3 to 5 years, it's a good idea to compile a list of games that are appropriate for different age groups. Also keep in mind disparities in income level among the families. Make suggestions for games that can be played with ordinary household items.

You can encourage families to play games with their children if you start a game library. The board games usually available in the game or math centers can be borrowed by families. Or teacher-made games can be packaged in tote bags and made available for family checkout. Many simple games can be photocopied and sent home for families to enjoy.

See also: **21   55   60–61**

27

Props for dramatic play can be found at thrift shops, yard sales, and flea markets and cleaned up for children's use. Some nifty career-related themes for prop boxes include architect, astronaut, baker, doctor, mechanic, firefighter, pharmacist, construction worker, and florist. Also collect props for different adventures: a day at the beach, a camping trip, planting a garden, a visit to a grocery store, and so on.

You can encourage families' involvement with prop boxes in two ways.

- Provide a list of items you need for prop boxes, so families can help gather the props. Also, invite parents to visit the class to tell about their jobs—and encourage them to bring items they wear and use at work. In some cases, these items or replicas of them can be used in prop boxes.

- As you develop a collection of prop boxes, make them available to families for use at home. This type of check-out system provides continuity between home and school and allows parents to observe the dramatic play that props encourage.

The Play-Full Prop Box

The ability to pretend is very important to a child's future success. To pretend, children must be able to recall experiences they have had and then re-create them. They must be able to picture experiences in their minds.

Children like to try on different roles, act out experiences, recall past events, and work out anxieties. One day a child may act out going to the grocery store, making a list, gathering items, paying at the checkout counter. Another day the child may pretend to be a dentist or a firefighter.

One way to encourage dramatic play—"pretend" experiences that enhance your child's cognitive abilities and encourage creative thinking and problem solving—is through the use of prop boxes or bags. Prop boxes contain an assortment of items centered on a dramatic play theme.

For a day-at-the-beach theme, a box may hold beach towels, old swimsuits, flip-flops, empty suntan-lotion containers, old sunglasses, and magazines. Or a box may contain a baker's hat, rolling pin, cookie cutters, playdough, pans, spoons, aprons, and dish towels.

Clearly label the containers, perhaps with pictures and words, and store them where your child can reach them. Keep adding to your collections. Yard sales and flea markets are great places to find props. As your child's interests change, start new collections.

Your child will benefit from these collections in many ways other than just having fun. For instance, research indicates that children who have many opportunities to participate in dramatic play use more sophisticated language and become better readers and writers.

Prop boxes are only as limited as the imagination.

Making Friends with Puppets

Valuable tools for the early childhood classroom, as well as great toys for your child at home, puppets have many uses with young children. They enhance spoken language, aid social play, promote prosocial behaviors, and allow children to express negative feelings without risk.

Puppets often help children relate to difficult situations by allowing them to identify with the puppet and still maintain an emotional distance. Kids who may not feel comfortable talking to an adult about personal problems might be willing to share those feelings with or through a puppet—either confiding to a puppet or assuming the puppet's character to express their feelings. For example, one child may tell a puppet, "When my mommy's not home, I get scared." But another child may slip on a puppet and have it say, "I know it's scary sometimes when Mommy is gone. When I get scared I talk to my friends, like I'm talking to you."

Adults who are sensitive to stresses a child may be experiencing can offer an appropriate puppet for the child to use. We can model the use of puppets, talking about feelings. If a puppet talks to children about his fear of the dark, kids who share that fear get the chance to work through their own fears.

The adult can have the puppet present the problem: "I'm so afraid when my daddy turns out the light at night! I don't like the dark. What should I do when Daddy turns out the light?" Children will offer the puppet suggestions: "You can have your daddy turn on a night light" or "You can ask your parents to leave the hall light on."

Puppets can be made, found at yard sales or flea markets, or purchased from toy stores, children's bookstores, museum shops—even department-store kitchen sections (where they are often sold as pot holders).

Sometimes it is hard to describe in writing a play situation and what children learn through different kinds of play. You can give parents a clear picture of young children's play through videotaping it. Show the video at an evening family meeting, commenting on children's actions or interactions at different points during the tape.

Videotaping is an effective way to help parents see what types of things children are learning as they play with puppets. After showing a videotape of children playing with puppets, ask parents what they saw in the children's play. Share your own comments to extend parents' awareness of the many kinds of development and learning that go on.

Parents can help create puppets either for the classroom or for their child's use at home. Have several puppet patterns available, along with the materials needed to make them. In less than an hour, parents can create several new puppets for the children to use in acting out familiar stories or in inventing stories of their own.

See also: **10 66**

29

We express the value we place on children's art by displaying their artwork. Mounting finger-painting pictures on coordinated construction paper and arranging them in a balanced display make children's art look like the true works of art they are.

Children can create their own art museum. Supply real picture frames or frames made from construction paper or poster board. Let each child decide which piece of art to frame. Display the artwork in a designated area of the room or in the hallway. Rotate artwork periodically as other works of art are completed.

Also encourage parents to display children's artwork in a prominent place at home: on the refrigerator door, in the family room or hallway, or on a special bulletin board.

Real Art for Real Children

We grown-ups provide the time, the space, the materials, and the atmosphere needed to create the wonderful works of art that only children can create. In valuing a child's first artistic attempts, however, we should appreciate the beauty of the color and design rather than worry about the finished product.

Real art for real children is

personal. Art can be as simple as colors representing a pretty day or as complex as a series of lives which express a sad feeling. It is important that each idea be developed by the child without adult preconceptions.

spontaneous. Always be ready for that creative moment!

inventive. Children need to have access to a variety of materials. Some art masters paint with egg yolks, mash berries for color, and use sticks for brushes. Experiment!

imaginative. Cows can be purple, tears gray with glitter. The moon really can smile, and mommies can have six arms.

unique. An original idea, combined with imaginative expression and materials of the child's choice, encourages ownership and a positive sense of self-esteem. No two works of art look the same when young children are the artists.

therapeutic. Art provides children with the means to gain control over their feelings. A completed creative work establishes feelings of self-satisfaction and self-confidence.

fun. Whether kids concentrate alone or work in a shared creative group, a positive, enthusiastic atmosphere of enjoyment is essential!

Creativity is Craftless

Remember when you attempted to put together your child's first instructions-enclosed, all-parts-included, no-batteries-required toy? So many steps had to be done a certain way that you had to refer to the instructions many times. And if you are like most of us, you felt uncertain, inept, and uncoordinated.

When a child is asked to duplicate a given pattern, following a series of steps that result in an end product, the same feelings emerge. Class craft projects may be cute to put in the family scrapbook or nice to send to Grandma, but they do little for your child's self-esteem, and cognitive development, and creativity.

That is why blank paper, scissors, paint, markers, glue, and a variety of other materials to choose from are available at all times in our classrooms. Children are encouraged to use the materials to make their own creations.

When we do a special art activity with children, we may introduce a new material or even demonstrate possible ways to use some tools and materials, but the children themselves decide what they want to create and how. The children care more, learn more, and enjoy an activity more when they produce their own creations—not copies of ours!

Many parents do not distinguish between a class craft project and a child's work of art. Some families have become so accustomed to children bringing home cute craft items that they fail to see the value in the messy finger painting a child proudly exhibits.

To help them understand the difference between the two activities, consider a bulletin board divided into two sections. On one side display craft items; on the other, open-ended works of art. Label each side and have small comments that point out the things learned by children through each type of activity.

Be clear in your own labels and language, too. Some teachers call craft activities "construction" because the children put pieces together to complete a product.

Over the course of a year you may chose to do a few craft-type activities—for instance, on a special occasion making simple frames for the children's own pictures. These activities have a limited place but should not be called "art." Art is open-ended with no specific end-product in mind; children are allowed to use materials in any way they choose.

See also: 6 11 29 31 85

31

In previous articles about literacy, we suggested that you highlight an author a week to expand your literacy program. To expand the book/art connection, you might focus on an illustrator instead. Collect books illustrated by a particular artist. After reading a book, point out colors and lines the illustrator used and identify the medium (watercolor, oil, chalk, ink, collage). Feature that medium in the art center, then display the children's artwork beside the work of the illustrator.

The Art of Books

You don't have to go to art galleries to appreciate beautiful artwork. Watercolor, oil painting, pen and ink, collage, and other forms of artwork can be found in quality children's literature. In our program we choose books not only for the stories they tell, but also for their wonderful artwork.

A trip to the library or bookstore offers the opportunity to compare the styles of different illustrators. Eric Carle, Tomie de Paola, and Ezra Jack Keats all have distinct artistic styles that even young children can learn to recognize with very little adult assistance.

Children enjoy experimenting with the art materials used by illustrators they know. One of their favorite artists, Stephen Gammell, illustrator of *Monster Mama*, *Old Henry*, and *Song and Dance Man*, uses watercolor and chalk to create splashes of color across the page.

Check out these books from the library and offer watercolors and chalk to your child. Create Gammell-like pictures together.

Extending literature in this way expands a child's horizons in many ways. But more than that, it's just plain family fun!

39 See also: **11 29–30 85**

Legos and Playdough— A Dynamic Duo

Children are not born with fine motor control. The process does begin early, when infants and toddlers reach for and grasp objects. But development and coordination of wrist and finger muscles—necessary for handwriting later—come slowly and require lots of practice.

Adults can help children develop fine motor control by providing appropriate materials. Playdough and Legos are two of the best materials.

One of the many skills learned through playing with playdough and Legos is the development of strength and dexterity in hands. Simply through pinching, rolling, and shaping playdough, children develop strength in finger and wrist muscles. Connecting Legos together develops hand muscles and the pincer grasp, the touching of the thumb and fingers that is important for holding pens, pencils, silverware, brushes, and other tools.

Playdough and Legos are both open-ended materials. Children can experiment with these however they choose. These materials not only help develop fine motor skills but also provide opportunities for practice and discovery of many math-related skills.

Playdough can be made at home or purchased. Legos are a considerable investment but worth it. Both materials provide hours of enjoyment, many ways to enhance fine motor skills, and great opportunities for intellectual development.

Along with the article, you might want to include this common recipe for making playdough.

1 cup salt

2 cups flour

1 teaspoon cream of tartar

2 tablespoons oil

2 cups water

a few drops of food coloring

Combine all ingredients in a pan and cook over low heat, stirring continuously, until all ingredients are well mixed and the dough begins to pull away from the side of the pan. The dough will look very lumpy but will mix smoothly after about 10 minutes of cooking. Remove from pan and knead for 2 minutes. The playdough can be reused for 3-4 weeks if kept in an airtight container.

As teachers, we can help parents recognize and build on children's interests as they develop fine motor skills. Keep a list of things that particularly interest each child and share it with parents at family conferences. For example, for a child fascinated by dinosaurs, playdough offers hours of modeling activity. Parents can also be on the watch for magazine articles, videos, and books on dinosaurs. For a child interested in spacecraft, Legos, Tinkertoys, or other building materials will provide hours of fun constructing the craft and imagining space adventures.

We can help families tune into their child's interests by knowing what children are interested in and what kinds of things they like to do. Equally important, parents can fill us in on interests children show at home.

See also: **23   33–35**

33

Children must have lots of experiences using scissors before they can be expected to cut accurately. In your classroom, have a basket filled with all kinds of paper that children can cut as they wish. Scraps of construction and tissue paper, ends of wrapping paper, wallpaper samples, leftover laminate, and discarded stationary and office memos can be cut into collage shapes for use in the art area. Children like to do this; they enjoy feeling useful.

Successful Scissoring

Have you ever wondered why young children have difficulty working with scissors? Managing scissors requires that a child combine fine motor skills—control and coordination of small muscles, especially hands, wrists, and eyes—with an intellectual task.

Closely related to motor development is physical growth and brain development. As the body grows physically and the brain develops, children are able to perform more intricate motor skills.

Most children are eager to cut with scissors. If a child is reluctant, it is probably because she is not ready.

A prerequisite to cutting with scissors is tearing, so we should allow young children many opportunities to practice tearing paper and materials such as lettuce and clay prior to teaching them how to use scissors.

In introducing kids to scissors, we first discuss safety rules and provide each child with appropriately designed scissors (initially with rounded points). So that we at school and you at home can work together on this skill, here is our approach to showing children how to use scissors.

Show them how to hold the scissors. Have them practice opening and closing the scissors several times before they try to cut paper. Show children how to hold the paper in one hand and the scissors in the other, to open the scissors and slip the paper between the blades, close the blades, then open them.

Let the children practice snipping small pieces of paper, old wrapping paper and greeting cards, and those catalogs and pieces of junk mail that you are recycling anyway. As the child develops proficiency, let him practice by cutting pictures from magazines, cutting along a straight line, and cutting along a curved line.

Puzzle Power

Puzzles help kids develop eye-hand coordination, an important skill. Learning to control their hands and fingers according to information received from their sight is a coordination skill that aids children in early attempts of reading and writing.

Three- or four-piece wooden puzzles, in which each piece fits into its own hole, are usually the first type of puzzle given to toddlers. As children mature and advance in their abilities to rotate pieces to match holes and find pieces that fit, they can handle increasingly complex puzzles.

Good quality puzzles usually are expensive but are a worthwhile investment because they can be used by many children, year after year. Also look for puzzles at yard sales, thrift shops, and toy lending libraries.

Homemade puzzles make great gifts. Appealing pictures, such as those in nature magazines or on holiday cards, can be mounted on cardboard and cut up for puzzles. Parents can look for pictures on topics of special interest to the child.

Children who are developing the ability to use scissors can use pictures from magazines to create their own puzzles. Making and playing with puzzles offer concrete experiences for young children to develop eye-hand coordination as well as cognitive skills.

With this article, you might include a request for parents to save old issues of nature, travel, home, or sports magazines. These come in handy during theme projects as children search for pictures of different seasons, various animal habitats, and the like. The magazines also are good for puzzle projects, for practice with scissors, and for just browsing.

See also: **23 32–33 35**

35

To Button, Zip, and Tie

Getting dressed on time in the morning can be a real challenge for many of us, but it is particularly difficult for young children who have to contend with buttons, zippers, and shoelaces when their fine motor skills are still developing.

When families are trying to get ready to leave the house at a certain time, parents will probably need to help young children with the dressing process. Preschool children want to be independent but get easily frustrated when the buttons won't do what they want them to do or the zipper will not cooperate. That frustration leads to an even more stressful morning.

Helping kids learn to contend with the logistics of buttoning buttons, zipping zippers, and tying shoelaces is best done during less stressful times. Concentrate on one skill at a time. Work together and assure children that they will be able to do this with practice. As a parent, you might want to consider shoes with Velcro fasteners, as well as other clothing items that young children can manage more easily as these skills are developing.

Learning to control hands and fingers according to information received from sight is a coordination skill that will aid children in early attempts of reading and writing.

We adults can provide many different opportunities for children to develop these skills. Dressing and undressing dolls and dramatic play with clothes that have buttons and zippers are good for practice. Activities such as shaping playdough, stringing beads, and placing pegs into pegboards also enhance the fine motor skills needed for dressing.

With appropriate experiences, your child will gradually master all the intricacies of getting dressed and undressed.

See also: **23 32–34 78**

Celebrations and Holidays

Some early childhood programs seem to build their curriculum around holidays, just going from one to the other on the calendar. We don't take that approach, but we do like to celebrate! We are just as likely to celebrate Dr. Seuss's birthday by enjoying *Green Eggs and Ham* (Random House 1976) as we are to celebrate Presidents' Day by reading *Just Like Abraham Lincoln* (Houghton Mifflin 1964).

We also honor the traditions of all the children and families in our program. We believe in the importance of family traditions and holidays in strengthening the connection between home and school.

As you know, upon enrollment, we gather information from families about the various heritages and traditions that make up our home-school community. With this knowledge, we plan activities to reflect the diverse cultures of our group and to foster respect for their cultures.

All preparations involve children in hands-on activities. Kids are invited to explore the special objects and foods that reflect different traditions.

We encourage each of you as families to join us in our celebrations. Even if you cannot be with us, please share your family traditions, recipes for holiday foods, and any special items that reflect your heritage and family history.

Because programs vary so much in the ways they respond to holidays, you will need to customize this article to your own practices and the reasons behind them. And if parents are part of the decision-making process with respect to holidays, you will want to add something explicit about their participation.

Some teachers and directors may choose to use this article early in the year or even hand it out at enrollment. Others may decide to use it a week or so before the first big holiday looms on the calendar.

See also: **9**

Toward Literacy ▶

Language and literacy development is often a major concern of parents with young children. These articles and accompanying activities are designed to help parents understand how a good early childhood environment promotes language and literacy through a variety of developmentally appropriate experiences. Parents also will find suggestions to enhance their own child's language development through poetry, writing, and reading experiences. By periodically sharing one of the articles with parents, you remind them of your goals and educational approach to children's development of language and literacy. Parents will be reassured that their child is on the road to proficient reading and writing.

As early childhood educators we know that children's language development is the foundation for their progress toward literacy. Children who are very fluent in oral language tend to have the easiest time learning to read, and they use their verbal skills in all areas of the curriculum.

Teachers can help parents understand how important it is to talk with children. But it isn't an easy thing for some parents to learn. Some parents instinctively chat with their children, but others have a hard time carrying on a conversation with a child; they have the habit of speaking to their children mostly to give orders.

Perhaps the most effective way of getting parents started on the conversation game is through modeling. When they visit the classroom or go on field trips with the group, parents see how teachers interact with children and how children respond. Watching videotapes of teachers engaged in conversation with children is useful, too.

After seeing a video, hearing a audiotape, or reading a brief exchange in print, parents could be asked to make a list of everything the child is learning or practicing. They will notice things they have never thought about before, and you can point out other learning that they have not recognized.

In such sharing with parents, be sure to communicate that there's no great secret or expertise in knowing what to say to children; it is not something that just teachers know how to do. *Anything* that parents say—a casual comment, question, or joke—gives children some raw material for their ongoing development of language.

Learning Language

Children begin very early in life to acquire language skills. Language helps children gain independence, interact with others, and participate in the surrounding culture. It plays a role in social interaction and expression of emotions, as well as learning.

Most children follow a sequence of language development: crying and cooing, babbling, first words, and first sentences. By the age of 5 most children have developed a proficiency in oral language and use it effectively to accomplish their purposes and meet their needs.

Even very young children are soothed by the mere voices of loved ones. Sing, chant, and carry on casual conversations with children—whether or not they answer or even before they are able to understand. Children tune in more than we sometimes realize. The language they hear is the raw material from which their own language develops—and through which much of their learning about the world takes place.

Kids learn a lot when adults simply talk to them in the course of daily activities such as cooking, bathing, and doing chores. Riding in the car or on a bus—or even pushing the shopping cart—parents can comment on what they see along the way. And there is a fringe benefit of keeping up running conversation: the child is less likely to get bored and to misbehave.

When you plan a family outing or special event, talk about it with your child beforehand and afterward. Anticipating and recalling experiences not only promote children's language development but also increase their knowledge and understanding.

Songs, fingerplays, and nursery rhymes are especially good for introducing children to the patterns and rhythms of language. And being read to is a real joy. When we take the time to read aloud and converse with our children, they learn to value language—as well as our company.

 See also: **38–40 44 46**

Fingerplays and Action Songs

Rhymes and movements for the hands and fingers, some of which date back almost 2,000 years, are still used in early childhood classrooms, as well as the more modern action songs that involve the whole body.

As children learn fingerplays and action songs, they learn the names of body parts, numbers, and shapes. The also learn other concepts and skills, including

- manual dexterity and muscle control;
- sense of rhythm of speech and music;
- new vocabulary;
- ability to follow directions;
- grasp of order and sequence;
- increased attention spans; and
- listening skills.

Fingerplays and action songs are a fun way to learn. They are a great way to pass a few minutes of transition time—while you are waiting in the car, in line at the grocery store, before or after dinner.

Children love repeating familiar rhymes, so come back to the same songs often enough that your child can learn the words of the rhyme and the movements that accompany the words.

Perhaps you remember a fingerplay from your childhood that you can share with us. If you would like to learn more fingerplays or action songs that are hits with kids of your child's age, just ask us—we'll be happy to share some great ones.

Include the words and movements for a few of the children's favorite fingerplays with this article. Encourage parents to share fingerplays that they remember from their childhood and include these in the newsletter for other families to enjoy.

Fingerplays and action songs help foster language. Let families know how much you value fingerplays by sending home a copy of each new fingerplay that children learn. Also send home a copy of the lyrics to new action songs.

Children, who often assume that their parents know everything, sometimes have trouble understanding why Mommy and Daddy don't know the words, say, to "Peanut Butter, Jelly." If you provide the words, parents can help children "remember" fingerplays and action songs at home.

See also: **39**

With this article, you might want to publish poems that the children have created. You might even print a special issue of the newsletter featuring children's poems and accompanying drawings. The poems may be written (or dictated) by the children during unit themes, on special subjects of interest, or by free choice. Or go one step further and compile a book of children's poems for the families to enjoy.

Make a point of gathering the work of poets from various nations and cultures, including (but not limited to) those in your program. The poetry of Maya Angelou and Eloise Greenfield, for example, has special gifts to offer to children, whatever their ethnic and cultural background.

Other aspects of families' lives and backgrounds can be reflected in your collection. In a rural setting, for example, look for poets such as Aileen Fisher who focus on country themes.

Consider providing a poetry shelf and encouraging parents to browse for a book to take home and enjoy with their child. A display board above the shelf could feature children's poems and responses to poems. Also provide families with copies of poems that you are reading aloud to children.

Rhythm and Rhyme

Poetry paints verbal pictures for children, tells them stories, and expresses emotions that they are feeling. Poetry is a unique use of language. From an early age children love hearing it read aloud.

The rhythm of poetry, and sometimes its rhymes, provide young children with the predictability that is important in their development and understanding of language and literacy. Poetry helps children develop auditory discrimination and it provides pleasurable listening experiences with sounds, repetition, and imagery. Kids particularly love nonsense verse and the marvelous sounds of poets like Dr. Seuss, Edward Lear, and A.A. Milne—and, of course, in the Mother Goose rhymes.

Here are a few suggestions for using poetry with your child.

- Provide a variety of poetry books.
- Help collect poems from birthday and other cards.
- Listen to songs that use poetry.
- Read aloud riddles and nursery rhymes.
- Engage in fingerplays together.
- Invite the child to illustrate poems that he or she particularly enjoys.
- Encourage creation of original poems—be available to take dictation.

Through the creative and meaningful use of poetry, children grow in language development. They—and you—can have a wonderful time in the process.

Getting It All Together

Think about how your child learned to speak. Did you teach your child one sound at a time to say, "I—need—to—go—pot—ty"? Of course not! Language is learned through listening, speaking, and practicing in real situations.

Children learn to read and write when real-life opportunities make learning fun and easy. In our classrooms, you may find the dramatic play area transformed into a restaurant, a bank, or an office. Such play presents a variety of opportunities for language use.

Paper and pencils are always available in every center to encourage children to attempt to make meaningful communications to their friends. Boys and girls may choose to communicate through drawings or paintings, in strings of circles or lines that imitate adult writing, or even in words that you can read.

Just as your child learned language in context from you and other people around her, kids are learning the beginnings of reading and writing in meaningful contexts here in the classroom.

We grown-ups encourage children's writing in many ways. "I love getting notes from you" or "This will help me to remember to buy more ice cream" or "Will you read me what you wrote?" says that we appreciate their efforts. What joy you and your child can share when she "reads" you her first written communication!

With this article, consider including examples of children's writing. Photocopy children's scribbles, strings of random letters, or invented spellings, and supply their translations of what they wrote. In this way you convey that you value the early stages of writing, just as you do the more advanced writing of elementary-school children.

All families want to help their children learn, but sometimes they don't realize that correcting children's speech or telling them that their scribbles aren't "real writing" is not helpful. When their speech is corrected frequently, children may become less verbal. When their early writing attempts are not valued, children may stop writing.

Sharing this article is a good way to begin a family meeting that focuses on how to support children's emerging oral language and early attempts at reading and writing. Distribute copies of this article as families arrive.

After parents have had a few minutes to read the article, ask them to share some stories about their child learning to talk. Then ask them what they did to "teach" their child how to speak. Few will have an answer, because not very many parents undertake a systematic effort to teach young children to talk.

Discuss how parents provided the appropriate environment as children learned to talk and how they respected children's early approximations of speech. Then explain how adults also can provide the appropriate environment for emergent literacy.

Give families specific suggestions about modeling reading and writing and about how they can respect children's early attempts at reading and writing.

See also: **14 37 41–53**

Perhaps you will want to include in each newsletter a piece that features children's writing. Or consider a special issue that focuses on writing, using as the lead this article or one of the others about writing. Personalize the column or newsletter by including writing samples from your class or various classes in the program. Include a piece about how adults in your setting model writing for children. Offer specific suggestions on types of writing that adults and young children can do together (some of these are listed in article no. 43).

Many adults remember their own early experiences with writing as endless practice with forming letters and daily copying from the board. Educators view writing very differently today; the focus in the writing curriculum for young children is communication. When very young children scribble on a piece of paper, we see that as the start of writing. When they write letters that they create on their own, these are seen as writing. Early childhood educators help families to understand this new view of writing and to value their children's early stages of writing.

"Mark-It Tips" for Young Writers

The motor skill required for writing began when your baby first grasped a rattle and continued to develop as she inspected dandelions between her thumb and forefinger. It takes lots of practice for fine motor control to develop. By the time your child was 2, holding a marker with her whole hand was possible.

Throughout the preschool years, children need frequent opportunities to work with an assortment of writing materials. Because the child's control of the small hand muscles is not yet very refined, large blank surfaces for drawing are very important. Try to offer several choices of white and colored paper, construction paper, and cardboard.

Provide markers, minimarkers, crayons, pencils with erasers, colored pencils, paints, and chalk—as many choices as you can. Variety keeps children experimenting with different writing tools and combinations of paper.

Not all experiences need to be on paper, however. Chunky pieces of chalk for drawing on the sidewalk are great. Later, house-painting brushes dipped in a bucket of water will easily get the chalk off the sidewalk. Activities like these help your child learn to write.

To encourage children to write, we always have paper and markers available. We are glad to see that children not only use them to draw but also put them to use in many other ways—from labeling a block structure they don't want anyone to knock down to putting price tags on items in their grocery store.

Stages of Children's Writing

Educators look at writing very differently than they did a generation ago. The things that young children seem to do naturally when given paper and markers are now viewed as true forms of writing. There are at least six different stages of writing:

Drawing. Children draw and "read" their drawings as a form of communication. They may draw an unrecognizable form and say, "I played in the home center today with my friends." Or they may draw a treelike form and say, "This says remember to take me to the park."

Scribbling. Young children believe they are writing when they scribble and often "read" what they have just scribbled. Children often will move the pencil like adults, making their scribbles from left to right.

Invented letters. Many young children make up their own letters. A circle with a line drawn down from the bottom (resembling a lollipop) is a common invented letter. Again, children believe they are writing.

Random letters. As children become more aware of the alphabet, they often write the letters in long strings, usually at random.

Invented spelling. Invented spelling takes many forms but is related to the sounds the child hears in each word. At the beginning of this stage, children may write one letter to represent one word. Later, words are represented by two letters, the initial and ending letter sounds. As the child's writing continues to mature, most sounds are represented in their invented spelling.

Common spelling. The child begins writing more and more words spelled as adults spell.

To illustrate the stages of writing, you can include samples collected from children in your program. You will also find the samples and simple descriptions useful for parent-teacher conferences. Comparing the child's writing samples, particularly over a period of months, helps families understand that the child is working toward conventional writing by experimenting with different types of emergent writing.

See also: **14 23 41 43 53–54**

Write Before Your Child's Eyes

Children learn about writing by observing people who already know how and by participating with those people in simple writing experiences. Parents and older siblings serve as models for children, showing them what writers do.

Kids are more likely to want to communicate in writing if they grow up in a home where they often see people writing. The more they see you writing, the more inclined they are to want to write.

As children begin "writing," they may use drawing, scribbling, or invented letters and spellings to express themselves. These are legitimate forms of early writing and to be encouraged!

Share your writing tasks with children. For example, include your child when you write out the weekly grocery list or jot down a reminder to yourself or another family member. And get the child to help with writing party invitations, thank-you notes, and cards or letters to relatives and friends.

When you have writing tasks to do—even something as humdrum as your to-do list—try to get in the habit of doing them when your child is around. Before you know it, you'll have an eager writer on your hands.

The Rewarding Ritual of Reading Aloud

Parents are children's first and most influential teachers. Reading together is one of the earliest shared experiences of parents and children. When you read a story to a child, you are her reading teacher.

Children learn to read by being read to. Research shows that early and good readers come from homes where reading is valued and experienced regularly. The desire to read starts with the early enjoyment of being held in a lap and cuddled as a story is read.

In addition to the feelings of warmth and security fostered by laptime reading, reading aloud to children expands their world and vocabulary. It creates an appreciation of the value of print, promotes knowledge of the mechanics of reading from the top to the bottom of the page and from left to right, and helps create an understanding of a sequence of events.

Setting aside time every day to read to your child says, "I love you and I want to spend special time sharing a story with you." It further demonstrates *your* love for books and sets the stage for developing in your child an interest and desire to become a reader.

Let your child pick a story. Then cuddle up together to enjoy exploring the power and magic of the printed word!

Research shows that one of the very best things familes can do for children's development and later school success is to read aloud to them. But making the time to read to children can be difficult nowadays, especially if families do not realize how important shared reading experiences are.

As early childhood educators, we can

- remind parents of the pleasures and benefits of reading with their children by including various reminders and tips in newsletters or other communications.

- send home a book with each child now and then. Inexpensive pocket folders, sized to hold most paperback books for young children, will protect the book from damage.

- help parents develop the habit of using the public library by providing library brochures (with maps, hours of operation, and services offered) from various branches that are convenient to families.

See also: **45–46 49 81**

Families sometimes need guidance in selecting books that are appropriate for their children. Regular listings of quality children's literature could be sent home—or added to your newsletter.

Y ou can help parents acquire children's books at very reasonable prices by sending home order forms from book clubs. Quality children's books can be ordered from Scholastic or Trumpet for under $3. The addresses for these book clubs are

Scholastic Book Clubs Inc.
2931 East McCary Street
P.O. Box 7503
Jefferson City, MO 65102-7503

The Trumpet Club
P.O. Box 604
Holmes, PA 19043

A Book of One's Own

Children are more likely to become avid readers if they have a few books of their own. There is a special pleasure—even for a young child—in being able to go to their own bookshelf and browse through favorite books.

Books can be expensive, though, especially if they are new and hardback. Paperback and used books are much less expensive yet just as cherished. Quality children's books, at very reasonable prices, often can be found at half-price bookstores, yard sales, thrift shops, or public library book sales. Take your time browsing and be choosy. The cost savings is worth the time it takes to look for good books.

Books make wonderful gifts. Tell grandparents and others that you welcome gifts of storybooks. And remember that when you buy a book for your child and read it together, you are laying a strong foundation for the child's lifelong learning.

See also: **31 47–48**

Read Me a Story—Again!

As they finish reading a storybook to a child, grown-ups often groan when they hear the words, "Read it again!" Many of us grown-ups tire of reading the same books over and over, but repeated reading is actually very good for young children.

Children learn important things from hearing a book again and again. They learn basic grammar and story structure. They also learn new vocabulary words and learn to associate the words with the illustrations on the page. In time, they will be able to tell the story themselves, using the visual clues of the illustrations.

Children who hear and retell stories refine their retellings until their memory of the words they have heard is so close to the text that they correct themselves as they "read" the story. Although their "reading" is primarily recitation rather than word identification, they gradually associate the text with the words they are saying.

As children incorporate stories into their memories, familiar words and phrases appear in their vocabulary. A child inspired by Bill Martin Jr.'s *Brown Bear, Brown Bear, What Do You See?* (Holt, Rinehart & Winston 1983) may ask a friend, "Tiffany, Tiffany, what do you see?" Or, having just read Eric Carle's *The Very Hungry Caterpillar* (Collins 1979) a child may say, "On Monday, I ate through one sandwich, but I was still hungry."

To develop into lifelong readers, children need opportunities to learn to love books. What better way than snuggling up as Mom, Dad, or another family member reads a favorite book—again?

Another way to provide opportunities for children to hear stories repeatedly is through the use of audiotapes and tape recorders. Audiotapes of many popular books and stories can be checked out of public libraries or purchased at local bookstores or through book clubs.

Adults and children also can make audiotapes of their own. Some of children's favorite tapes are those they helped to record. Consider recording a few audiotapes of children reading familiar books—or just joining in on the repeated parts of books—and making those tapes available for family checkout.

You could put a small box in each newsletter that gives families specific ideas about  *how to extend books. Great ideas can be found in Story S-t-r-e-t-c-h-e-r-s by Shirley Raines and Robert Canady (Gryphon House 1989).*

The following four articles discuss ways to extend reading in the home. Books take on added value when parents and children make their own books or share planned experiences related to books they've read. Some families may not think about ways of "extending" books unless you help them see the possibilities and benefits.

Book Projects

Written language is acquired by children in many of the same ways they acquire oral language. Two crucial aspects of learning oral language are having opportunities to be a language user and having adult role models.

We can engage children in the exploration of written language by writing with them. Written communication is tied to reading. For the family who enjoys books, many opportunities will present themselves for book projects.

For example, after reading a story about a family, you might suggest making a family book together. You can discuss with the child whom to include in the book, how big the book should be, what shape to make it, and how many pages it should have. The child can decide how to depict family members (in drawings, photographs, or other means), as well as what to write and how to design the cover.

Another opportunity arises when your child makes up a story or tells you about something he did with his class. Perhaps he would like to make his story into a book. If so, he can dictate the words to you or do the writing himself—in his own way, whatever that is—and add pictures.

By providing an accepting, encouraging, and stimulating environment, we foster in children a strong self-image and positive attitude toward writing and reading.

57 See also: **40 42 48–49**

Make Your Own Storybooks

Children love stories and love making things, so take advantage of this terrific combination and make some books with your child. Preschool children are ready to help write and illustrate stories from their own experiences or imaginations.

Here's an idea.

1. Write down a story as your child tells it. Be sure to write the child's words, not yours, and repeat the words as you write. This process helps a child recognize that print is "talk" written down.

2. Place an appropriate number of words at the top of separate pages and reread the story with your child.

3. Invite your child to illustrate each page and, if she wishes, to create a cover, title page, and dedication.

4. Arrange pages in order and place in a notebook.

5. Encourage your child to "read" this new book to you.

This same process can be used with photographs that describe a trip to the zoo, a vacation, or a visit from Grandma.

These unique books make wonderful gifts. You might want to photocopy them (color photocopies are great!) and give them to several members of the family or close friends.

Remember, whatever the topic, we adults act only as the scribes for the child's words and as assistants in putting the book together. Children should make all the decisions about the content and creation of their own storybooks!

See also: **42 47 49**

49

Bringing Books to Life

Books should be an integral part of a child's life. You can bring books to life for your child by finding books that relate to the family's activities and by extending books that you've already read together.

Books about family activities are relatively easy to find. For example, if you go to the zoo, find a book about animals; if you walk along a park pond, get a book from the library that discusses pond life; if you have a new baby, find a book about infants and siblings. The possibilities are endless.

Ask a children's librarian or someone who works in the children's section of a bookstore to help you find books of interest. Look for other books at used book sales or yard sales and flea markets.

Extending a book the family has already read is easy, too. It's as simple as providing materials for children to draw or paint their favorite part of the book.

Or you can act out what the characters in a book do. If the characters are firefighters or astronauts or chefs, gather a few props to spark the child's play. If the characters plant a garden, you and your child can, too. If the story or a part of it takes place at a bakery or grocery store, in a forest, or at a swimming pool, read it just before you set out for the same kind of place. Then, with your child you can notice things you saw in the book, point out things you haven't seen before, and look at the book again when you get home.

When children read about familiar activities or when they act out favorite stories, books comes alive for them. Reading becomes more meaningful, more memorable, and more fun.

Booking and Cooking

When we cook in class, children combine ingredients, mix, stir, and taste. They also use the descriptive words of literature—nouns, verbs, adjectives, and adverbs—to describe the what, how, where, and why, as well as the movements, textures, tastes, and feelings, associated with food and cooking.

This combination of cooking and books can be continued at home. As Sunday morning pancakes are cooked, consider referring to Eric Carle's *Pancakes, Pancakes* (Simon & Schuster 1990) or Tomie de Paula's *Pancakes for Breakfast* (Harcourt Brace Jovanovich 1978). Make split pea soup from the *George and Martha* series by James Marshall (Houghton Mifflin) or porridge after reading a version of *Goldilocks and the Three Bears*. Buy or bake different kinds of bread after you read *Bread, Bread, Bread* by Ann Morris (Mulberry 1989).

Literature and cooking experiences are limited only by your imagination. Use your child's food preferences as a starting place and expand the experiences from there.

As in any other shared reading time, talking about the story is just as important as reading the book. Make comments about the plot as you read, helping connect events in the book to the child's life. For example, when reading *The Very Hungry Caterpillar* by Eric Carle (Collins 1979), you might remark, "Remember when we bought those good plums at the grocery store?" Ask questions that help your child think about the story: "How do you think you would feel if you ate everything that the Very Hungry Caterpillar ate on Saturday?"

Connecting books with enjoyable family experiences—like cooking or conversation—sends your child the message that reading is fun for children and grown-ups, too.

Few experiences are as much fun for children as cooking, and cooking offers lots of opportunities for connections to books. With your help, parents will see how hands-on experiences like cooking can make books even more special to children.

Give parents specific ideas about books with a link to cooking. Here are some ideas:

- *Green Eggs and Ham* by Dr. Seuss (Random House 1976): colored eggs and ham
- *The Gingerbread Boy* by Paul Galdone (Houghton Mifflin 1975): gingerbread
- *Blueberries for Sal* by Robert McCloskey (Viking 1948): blueberries or blueberry tarts
- *Jamberry* by Bruce Degen (HarperCollins 1983): toast or muffins and jam
- *Anansi and the Moss-Covered Rock* by Eric Kimmel (Holiday House 1988): fruits and vegetables
- *Chicken Soup with Rice* by Maurice Sendak (Scholastic 1976): chicken soup

See also: **25** **49**

All parents want their children to learn to read. But many have heard about strategies to help children learn letters or words, such as drilling with flashcards, that are not suited to the way young children learn best.

The following three articles describe appropriate activities through which families support children's emergent literacy and prepare them for conventional reading. When you model these activities with children in your program, parents see that you value this approach.

During family meetings, point out the environmental print in your room and explain the labeling process. Consider letting parents know what labels and other kinds of environmental print have been added to the room each week. Suggest that parents look for similar environmental print or label similar items at home.

Letter Learning

Learning the names of alphabet letters—like all early learning—is best done in the context of what is meaningful to young children.

Many children first learn the initial letter of their own name, which has a great deal of meaning and importance to them. For the child who loves jello, *J* may be an important letter, while the child who knows that Daddy works at the Texaco station may begin to notice the letter *T*.

Some children learn to read without knowing the names of letters or the sounds associated with them. But research shows that for most children, associating names and sounds with the alphabet comes before conventional reading.

However, this finding does *not* mean that letter names should be drilled into young children. There are far more effective and enjoyable ways for children to learn about letters. For instance, children enjoy labeling items that they choose. Sound out the name of the object together to determine which initial letter to use, then cut out big letters from magazines or newspapers and invite the child to tape them on items that she wants labeled.

At home or out together, point out letters and words that are likely to be of special interest to your child. Try simple activities such as reading logos of favorite foods and stores, identifying street signs, writing grocery lists together, and playing with magnetic letters on the refrigerator door while singing the alphabet song. Remember, children learn through play!

 See also: **52–54**

Entering the World of Words

Print surrounds us. In our homes we have mail, newspapers, magazines, books, and various boxes and cans of food. When we drive down the highway, we encounter traffic signs, billboards, and signs that identify stores. At the grocery store we see advertising and logos.

Children begin to make sense of this print in their environment very early in life. Any parent who has driven down the street and heard their toddler cry out, "French fries!" or "Stop, Mommy!" knows that the child is finding meaning in that big M that signals a certain fast-food restaurant.

Children often recognize the name of the grocery store or drug store where they go with their parents to shop. When children's attention is called to the logo and the name of the store is shown to them, they are likely to remember it.

The same is true of a child's favorite foods. Toddlers can tell Fruit-Loops from Cheerios. Initially, children use the logo for clues as to what the words say; they, for instance, will occasionally "read" the word *Crest* as *toothpaste*. This is normal when children are first learning to make sense of the print they see.

Parents can begin making children aware of environmental print very early on. In doing so, they help their children establish important reading skills.

See also: **51   53–54**

Label It, Learn It

As you enter your child's classroom, you discover the door has been labeled with a sign that says *Door* and the wall is labeled *Wall*. What is going on?

When young children begin to associate the name of an object with that object, they start to realize that words have meaning and power. From their first realization that saying "water" gets them a drink and that "outside" lets other people know they want to play outdoors, children use the spoken word to get what they need and want.

The next step is to begin to associate letters and words with objects. One way we introduce this idea is by labeling objects in the room.

This link can easily be made at home, too. Just remember to keep it simple and label only a few things at a time.

- Begin with signs that incorporate only one letter—wear one that says M for Mother or D for Dad. Let your child watch as you print the letter.
- Wear signs or stickers that announce your first names.
- Label those objects your child asks you to label.
- Encourage your child to make his or her own signs to display around the house.

While the labels are posted around your house, talk with your child about them. Find other things that begin with the same letter sound.

When children see the same labels day after day, they have a tendency to tune them out. So as they seem to lose interest in some labels, make new ones.

 See also: **51–52 54**

Whole Language *or* Phonics? No, It's Both!

You may have heard the complaint that a whole-language approach means not teaching phonics. Don't believe it! Just about everyone agrees that children should learn phonics. The question is only whether young children should be taught phonics as a memorized set of sound/letter connections *before* they begin learning to read.

As we see it, there are various skills and understandings that children develop in moving toward becoming readers. What seems to work best is for kids to develop these simultaneously—phonics included—through experiences that are meaningful to them.

In our program we plan a wealth of experiences to spark children's interest in learning to read and write and to acquaint them with various skills and knowledge that they need to do so. Here are a few of the things we do.

- Read favorite stories and poems again and again, making sure the children can see the text and pointing to words as we say them so kids begin to make sound/letter associations.

- Involve children in making charts that show sound/letter patterns of special interest to them—for example, words that start the same way as each child's name or words that rhyme with our hamster's name.

- Encourage children to use their own invented spellings for representing the sounds of words, which helps them develop their phonics sense as well as their writing—later they will move to conventional spellings.

See also: **14 37 51–53**

Math and Science

The articles in this section, as well as suggestions for parent communications, clarify the vital role of math and science in an early childhood program. As parents read the articles or participate in the suggested activities, they will become more aware of how children learn math and science concepts through hands-on experiences with real materials and daily opportunities for exploration. They will realize how much children learn—math-wise and science-wise—by participating in household tasks, family outings, and other such experiences.

55

For many adults, math conjures up the memory of workbook pages and flashcards. Parents may try to give their children an edge in math by coaching them on counting numbers or by drilling simple addition facts; they also may worry when the teacher does not do these things. Such rote learning has little to do with real understanding of mathematical concepts, but many parents do not realize this.

Teachers and directors need to share with families how children actually develop mathematical understanding and skills. The math articles in this section can be used to help parents feel comfortable with today's hands-on approach to math, but the written word should only be a part of your efforts to communicate.

One of the most effective ways to support parents' understanding of your program's math curriculum and teaching methods is for families to experience math the way their children do. Plan a Math Night for families. Invite parents to experience the kind of "math moments" mentioned in the adjacent article and to explore various math manipulatives. Have them solve simple problems: measure a table with linking cubes, sort pattern blocks by color and shape, or use colored counters to see how many people in the room like bananas better than grapes.

Highlight math concepts in other learning centers. Let parents see how easily math can be applied to practical, real-life problems. The investment of an hour or two in an evening meeting could change family attitudes about math.

Continue to reinforce today's approach to early childhood math by giving families specific suggestions about activities that augment their efforts to provide an appropriate math background.

Math Moments

In every classroom, at any time during the day, the potential for a "math moment" exists. The room is one big learning center where strands of mathematical discovery are continually being woven. Children learn to make sense of their world through everyday experiences.

To stimulate a math moment, teachers use a variety of materials and ideas to create an environment in which children explore math concepts. In the math center are board games, puzzles, matching and guessing games, dominoes, cards, pattern blocks, and collections of objects that give children opportunities to recognize numbers and build math skills.

But math moments do not occur only in the math center. Look around our room. In block play, children construct cities (by sorting and organizing) and use words like *long, short, small,* and *tall.* At snacktime a child passes out one napkin per child and the same number of crackers for each person. We take attendance and keep track of how many days we've been in school. When the class takes a vote on what stories to read or for some other decision, children compare quantities.

Parents can accept the challenge to find math moments at home and about town. With your child, identify numbers and shapes in your junk mail. As you cook or do errands together, you can make comments or ask questions that encourage meaningful math understandings. For instance, "We need a bottle of juice for each person in the family and your friend Sally, too. How many shall I get?" Children love to be consulted on such issues. Just keep it all in fun!

 See also: **18–19 25–26 56–64**

The Shape of Things

Shapes are all around us, in natural objects, architecture, signs, and even in the numerals and letters we use. Shape knowledge underlies algebra, geometry, and other domains of higher mathematics.

This complex knowledge begins with the very simple foundation of recognizing simple shapes—circles, squares, triangles, ovals, rectangles, and diamonds. Children can begin to notice these shapes in the world around them, and you can help them to do so.

As you walk or drive along together, point out shapes you see in signs, rooftops, and windows. Involve the child in shape-spotting games: *Who can find the first triangle? How many shapes can we find in that building? Can you find two oval letters on that billboard?* You'll find that your child enjoys getting "in shape"!

To customize this article, you might photograph children's explorations with shapes and reproduce the photos in the newsletter. For example, take a picture of children with their block constructions or snap them as they create their own snacks with crackers in geometric shapes and cheese cut by cookie cutters. Sketches of children's creations or the children's own drawings are possibilities, too.

Involve families in helping their children begin to recognize basic geometric shapes in the world around them. One way to do this is through a class or center bulletin board.

Place one of the basic shapes in the middle of the board. Work with the children to take photographs of items that have that basic shape; then invite families to add to the collection with photographs from magazines.

For example, a large rectangle may be surrounded by photographs of

- a fish aquarium,
- the door of one of the classrooms,
- windows,
- tables,
- unit blocks,
- a computer keyboard, and
- the doll bed from the home center.

Ideas for such shared bulletin boards are innumerable. Inviting this type of family involvement does not require much time on the part of staff or families but fosters continuity between home and school.

See also: **12 32–34 55 57–58**

When you keep families informed of patterns their children are recognizing in school, they are encouraged to reinforce this learning at home. As children investigate patterns in the classroom, keep a list of the patterns they explore. Place this list where parents can see it, and from time to time include the list in the newsletter.

Seeing patterns is essential throughout mathematics. It also supports children's preparation for reading; readers see patterns in words, repeated phrases, and story plots. And in other curriculum areas such as music and dance, the visual arts, and science, patterns are pervasive.

Use patterning as an example to help parents see the integrated nature of young children's learning—how a skill or understanding in one curriculum area is linked to other areas. Patterns exist in math, literacy, and in the natural world.

Picking Up Patterns

The ability to reproduce and create patterns is an early math skill that we adults can encourage in young children. Patterns occur throughout mathematics, but children's first experiences with patterns are with objects rather than numbers.

Children between 3 and 5 begin to be able to reproduce a pattern created by someone else. For example, if an adult uses blocks to create the pattern of rectangle, square, rectangle, square, and so on, the child will be able to look at that pattern and use his own blocks to make the same pattern.

Almost any set of objects around the house can create a simple alternating pattern (ABAB):

- spoon, knife, spoon, knife;
- blue napkin, red napkin, blue napkin, red napkin;
- nut, bolt, nut, bolt; or
- crayon, marker, crayon, marker

After children perceive and create this simple patterning, adults can offer more complicated patterns, such as nut, nut, bolt, nut, nut, bolt (AABAAB) or nut, nut, bolt, bolt, bolt, nut, nut, bolt, bolt, bolt (AABBBAABBB).

Encourage children to create their own patterns with objects. Ask them to predict which object would come next in one of your patterns. Invite them to sketch their patterns.

Finding patterns in the world around them and creating patterns themselves will help children see patterns in more complex mathematics later on.

69 | *See also:* **12 55–56 58**

Sorting Stuff

Children learn many math skills long before they are ready for the basics of addition and subtraction. One of these skills is the ability to sort objects.

When they sort, children group things that belong together in some way. Kids often sort by color—red blocks in one group, blue blocks in another—or by shape—triangle blocks here, rectangle blocks there.

When children's rooms are organized, their toys become natural objects to sort. At cleanup time, alphabet blocks go into one container, colored blocks into another, farm animal figures in one tub, and toy cars into a box.

In helping with the laundry, children can sort clothes into piles of shirts, shorts, pants, underwear, and socks. After dishes are done, kids can put away knives, forks, and spoons. In helping to put away groceries, children can divide boxes from cans or bathroom items from kitchen items. By lending a hand in sorting things into the appropriate recycling containers, children also develop earth-friendly habits.

Early in the child's explorations of sorting activities, adults play a useful role by providing words for what the child is doing ("I see you are putting all the square blocks together"). We also can help extend the sorting ("Let's see if we can find all the rectangle blocks"). In time the child begins to use these words and expand his or her understanding of the mathematical world.

Expand families' sorting activities by letting them know about classroom collections and encouraging them to begin their own. These could be collections of virtually anything: rocks, coins, shells, leaves, even labels from canned foods.

Such collections are interesting undertakings for families. Grouping and regrouping items in the collection offer multiple opportunities for sorting.

With support, children can develop several different categories or rules for their sorting activities.

- Rocks might be sorted by size, type, or texture.
- Coins can be sorted by type or year minted.
- Shells or leaves might be grouped by size, shape, color, markings, or type.
- Food labels can be sorted by color, content (vegetables or fruits), or manufacturer.

These ideas could accompany the article in a newsletter or be posted on a bulletin board.

See also: **12 25 31 34 55–57 59**

Use this article in a newsletter with several anecdotes about "math moments" that have occurred in the classroom during the past few weeks. Families love reading about their children and their children's friends. Stories about specific activities and new materials, accompanied by the children's reactions or comments, will keep parents posted on what's happening in the classroom. You also could suggest that families reinforce math concepts through children's books. Many good counting books can be read aloud during evening storytimes. These include

59

- 1, 2, 3 to the Zoo *by Eric Carle (Philomel 1988),*
- Animal Babies 1-2-3 *by Eve Spencer (Raintree 1990),*
- Each Orange Had 8 Slices *by Paul Giganti Jr. (Green-willow 1992),*
- How Many Snails? *by Paul Giganti Jr. (Greenwillow 1988),*
- Over in the Meadow *by Olive A. Wadsworth (Viking Kestrel 1985), and*
- The Icky Bug Counting Book *by Jerry Pallotta (Charles-bridge 1992).*

Counting Doesn't Add Up to Math

Sometimes we tend to think too simplistically about mathematics and young children. You hear someone say, "My daughter knows all her numbers. She can count to 20." While counting is an accomplishment, it is only one very small part of knowing numbers.

Counting to 10 or 20, or even 100, is called rote counting and requires only the memorization of number order. The child may or may not have any real understanding of amount or quantity.

Number vocabulary and concepts that young learners can begin to use in meaningful ways include *some, more, less, bigger, smaller, pairs, groups, parts,* and *wholes.* Talking and thinking about numbers and quantity as a part of doing activities is a natural way for children to develop mathematical concepts.

Parents can point out math-related aspects of everyday situations. Use number words in conversation: "Let's put these two shirts here" or "I need three more glasses on the table." Estimate how long it will take to get to Grandmother's house. Measure how far the ball rolls. Divide a dozen cookies among four family members.

A simple math vocabulary grows from experiencing cooking and measuring, understanding that numbers have names and written symbols, guessing and estimating, and talking about days and weeks. These experiences lay the groundwork for beginning math.

Parents play an important part in building children's initial math understandings. Look for ways to help kids see the fun and usefulness of knowing more than how to count to 100.

See also: **25 55 60–61**

"Playing the Numbers" in Kids' Games

Games are a wonderful way for children to learn and have fun at the same time. In matching and lotto games, children learn new vocabulary as they name the objects in the pictures. In board games, they develop an understanding of numbers as they determine how many spaces they can move by counting the dice dots or by recognizing the number on the spinner. In simple problem-solving games, children develop their reasoning ability and realize that many answers can be "right."

Playing games helps children learn to follow directions and take turns with others. Games provide opportunities to learn social skills with other children and adults.

Young children learn games best in a small group where they do not have to wait very long for a turn. They should begin playing simple games with clear instructions and those based more on chance than strategy or skill.

We should not insist that kids follow the rules all the time; if a child creates his own rules, play along. After all, having fun together is the main idea.

Keep up with games that are being produced commercially for children, and be honest with parents about what you think about these games. Some games advertised for preschool children are not appropriate for them. Be prepared to make specific game suggestions, and let parents know what children can learn in playing these games with their family or friends.

Card games that young children enjoy include Go Fish, Crazy Eights, Animal Rummy, and Old Maid. They also like lotto and domino-type games, as well as games of memory and matching, such as those based on Concentration.

Among the board games and other types of games appropriate for young children are Candyland, Chutes and Ladders, Hi-Ho Cherry-O, Connect Four, Guess Who, Checkers, and Othello.

See also: **26 55 59 61**

61

S *ending this article home or using it in your parent newsletter is most effective after children have learned several simple games with dice and cards. Along with the article, you can add the rules of the games you have been playing in class. You also could include a few quotes from the children or observations about their play.*

Here are some simple games you can start with.

Find the Diamonds—*Place a deck of cards face down, then turn over one card at a time. If the card is a diamond, say, "I found a diamond," and place it in the diamond pile. If the card is not a diamond, put it in the discard pile.*

Looking for Pairs—*Divide the deck into two stacks. Spread out one stack face up in a grid pattern. Stack the other cards together. Turn over the top card from this stack and look for a pair in the grid. When you find two cards with the same number, say, "I found a pair."*

Stack All the Suits—*Lay all four aces face up, side by side. Turn over the other cards one at a time and put them in the correct stack, depending on the suit: heart, diamond, spade, or club (or the variations of these suits that are used in cards designed especially for children).*

These games are very simple but can be great fun for young children, especially when they are able to play with teachers or parents.

Dice, Cards, and Math

Dice and playing cards are inexpensive, fun to work with, and suitable for a variety of math activities. They help children learn one-to-one correspondence, comparison of numbers, and other math skills.

Dice can be used in very simple ways, such as by players rolling a single die and advancing on a game board. Such games often can be purchased secondhand or created by families at home.

A piece of posterboard can serve as the game board. A child can select a starting place and ending place for the game. For example, for a game simply called Going to the Park, HOME can be the starting place, boxes can be drawn along streets, and PARK can be the destination. A game of this kind promotes number recognition and counting skills.

For older children, more advanced games can involve rolling two or more dice and adding (or subtracting) the numbers shown. Dice also can be used to help children look for number patterns and factors by finding all the ways to make a certain number on a pair of dice.

Dice do not need to be six-sided. Game and hobby stores sell dice with 4, 8, 10, 12, 20, even 100, sides! And for young children, incomplete decks of cards are just as much fun as complete decks—just be sure that every card has a match.

Playing cards, too, offer many possibilities for math games. Children can play War or other games that involve a comparison between two or more numbers. They can count decks to determine how many cards are red, how many are hearts, how many are face cards, how many are less than 7, and so on. Such games and others like Animal Rummy or Go Fish teach children about grouping and sorting.

Families also can create their own card games. If your family invents a game that is fun, we'd love to hear about it.

See also: **26 55 57 59–60**

Do Birds Have Ears?

Young children are naturally curious and enjoy exploring the world around them; they find countless things to observe, investigate, and wonder about. *Why does a spider spin a web? Do birds have ears? How do fish breathe?*

Parents and teachers can foster children's natural curiosity in many ways. When a child expresses an interest in a subject or poses a question about a natural phenomenon, a trip to the library can reveal answers and open up other doors to learning.

Family outings—even simple, short, inexpensive excursions—pique children's interest in the natural world. Parents and children encounter many wonders on walks through the park, along a pond, even in a neighbor's vegetable garden. Other visits can be planned to nature centers, science museums, zoos, fossil-laden hills, beaver dams—the choices are endless.

From time to time, pack a picnic lunch and make a day of it. Be sure to take along a couple of containers (at least one with air holes in it) so that you and your child can collect specimens. An inexpensive magnifying glass is also a valuable field accessory. And don't forget paper and pencils.

Talk about what you see. Your child might like to draw some observations. Encourage her questions by writing them down in a notebook for further investigation—most of us find that we don't know the answers to all of kids' questions, and it's fun to research them together. The child's curiosity and spirit of investigation thrive when you are her fellow scientist, wondering about things and checking them out together.

The following three articles are about science: the tasks of observing, asking questions, experimenting, and learning new information.

Through a parent checklist or in informal conversation, you can find out about parents' hobbies, interests, and areas of expertise. On class field trips, it's good to have along an expert or enthusiast to comment on discoveries and to answer questions that come up. For instance, maybe one of the parents is a naturalist, willing to spend a few hours with the children on a visit to the zoo.

Special show-and-tell days or weeks could be set up for parents so they can share stories, artifacts, and discoveries with the children at their convenience.

See also: **20 63–64 82 89**

Consider including, in the newsletter or on a bulletin board, photographs of children investigating the world of science. Capture them as they plant seeds, hold a rabbit, experiment with a magnet, or examine a worm. Include questions or comments that children come up with during these experiences.

Science by Discovery

Children learn scientific concepts through real experiences such as playing in the mud, holding a rabbit, walking in the rain, jumping into leaves, and playing with worms. For young children, science is a natural and spontaneous process—and sometimes a messy one! Teachers and parents can enhance children's understanding of science by allowing kids to "mess around" in the physical world.

Our program promotes the development of the processes that are integral to science: observing, classifying, communicating, measuring, inferring, and predicting. Observation skills are learned by examining rocks and leaves or by noticing the different sizes of shadows. Classifying skills are learned through sorting buttons or shapes and by recognizing similarities and differences of objects.

Children develop measurement concepts and skills by measuring how much a plant has grown or by using blocks to measure their friends' height. Finally, children infer and predict outcomes by guessing what is inside a box or by predicting what will happen when water is poured over ice. These are examples of ways in which science is used every day.

Including children in preparing supper, planting a flower bed, or building a bookshelf provides additional opportunities for children to experience science firsthand. A young child's natural curiosity and willingness to explore new things make the preschool years the perfect time for beginning the science curriculum.

See also: **18–20 62 89**

Reap the Rewards of Gardening

Gardening allows children to plan and work together to create something they believe is important, and it allows teachers to integrate all curriculum areas: reading, writing, math, and science.

Similar experiences can be shared at home. A garden need not be extensive or have dozens of kinds of plants. A barrel, a window box, or cut-in-half gallon jugs do nicely.

Even young children can do "research" to find out what kinds of plants might grow best in their backyards or in containers. Parents can take children to libraries and local greenhouses to find out what to plant and how to take care of those plants. Or kids can ask family friends and neighbors about their gardening experiences.

Math skills are apparent throughout the gardening process: counting the seeds, measuring the correct distance between plants, marking the calendar for the anticipated date of seedling appearance, measuring the height of the plants as they grow. Science lessons emerge as the plants grow and as beneficial and harmful insects make their appearances.

Reading and writing skills are enhanced when books about gardening are read to children and when kids draw pictures and write stories about their own plants. *The Little Red Hen* by P. Galdone (Clarion 1973) and *The Carrot Seed* by Ruth Krauss (Harper & Row 1945) are two of the many books that help stimulate kids' interest in gardening.

Another plus is that children develop a sense of responsibility for their gardens. They feel a true sense of pride and accomplishment as their plants grow bigger and bigger and as they share their harvest.

Whether your center is in a rural area with a gardening tradition, or in an urban area where community gardens are popular, find some nearby spot where children can sow and reap the rewards of a garden. Even if a potential plot cannot be found, a container garden on the playground makes a fine alternative.

A vegetable garden is the perfect opportunity to get parents involved. Check your list of family interests/hobbies to see if some parents are gardening enthusiasts. Ask them to drop by for a planning meeting—to determine how much space is available, what grows best in your area, where tools can be kept, how the harvest will be shared, and other specifics.

Then, to gauge further interest, run a short newsletter blurb or produce handouts that announce the garden and invite all parents to lend a helping hand. With the proper planning, only an initial meeting will be necessary. Families then can tend the garden at their convenience.

As a companion project, consider a compost pile. Families can contribute grass clippings and kitchen waste. The garden will benefit from the nutrient-rich mulch, and children and adults alike will learn about the benefits of recycling. You could ask one or two parents to volunteer to tend the compost heap.

See also: **62–63 89**

Social-Emotional Development ▶

In these articles we seek to help parents understand the social and emotional development of the young child. By describing how the program deals with a variety of issues, from helping children get started socially to dealing with troublesome behaviors, teachers and directors provided much-needed reassurance and help build trust. Parenting suggestions, especially on discipline issues, are also welcome. The articles and activities can serve as a springboard for further communication between staff and parents.

"Off to a Good Start" should be given to parents well before the child begins the program. In year-round programs it can be included in the packet of materials parents receive at enrollment. In nine-month programs, including the article in a summer mailing or newsletter gives parents the opportunity to read and think about the child's transition to the new setting long before the first day arrives.

You will want to add information specific to your program—for example, where to park, rules about signing the child in, and the like. This will help the family feel more prepared and more at ease as well as make the child's first day less stressful. It is helpful, too, for teachers to make a home visit before the child begins the program.

Having given much thought to the first few days of school, you may have specific plans to ease the transition for children, such as beginning with a shorter day, using a phase-in schedule (e.g., half of the children coming the first day, the other half the next, and then the whole group), or having parents participate for the first hour. Of course, you will want to inform parents in advance of any such procedures and expectations for the first days of school. In particular, are parents allowed or encouraged to stay for part or all of the first day? What about subsequent days? Will they be participating? What do you suggest when they leave?

Off to a Good Start

Do you remember your first day at nursery school or kindergarten? You probably were nervous and excited—and a bit lonely and lost when your mom or dad left. Even when returning to a familiar setting after summer vacation, children usually feel a bit intimidated. They may have a new teacher, there are new kids in the group, and maybe that special friend is gone. It's a big deal!

We want to do everything we can to make your child's beginning here as happy as possible. The parent packet is designed to fill you in on specifics. If you haven't yet visited the program with your child, we encourage you to come in before the child's first day. Usually a visit when the program is *not* in session is less overwhelming; the child can look around the room, get acquainted with us, and just get the feel of the place.

Before the program starts, you may want to read your child a few books with a starting-school theme. Such stories can help the child get in touch with her feelings about going into a new place and separating from you. Reading also gives the child an opportunity to talk about feelings or ask questions about what to expect.

It's also a good idea to go over our daily schedule with the child, talking about some of the things she'll be doing in the course of the day. Some children feel a little less alone and adrift in a new place if they bring along something familiar from home, such as a favorite stuffed animal or even a family photo.

And on the first day, be sure to arrive in plenty of time. In fact, if your child tends to have a tough time in new groups, make a point of coming early the first few days so we can help her get involved in something fun, perhaps with one or two other children, before the crowd arrives.

Finally, when it's time to leave, don't slip out when your child isn't looking. Children need to know when you're going and be able to say goodbye. Don't worry. We'll take it from there.

 See also: **68** **75**

Helping Children Cope with Stress

Any major change in a child's life can cause stress. Common sources of stress are the birth of a new sibling or the divorce of parents. Stress also can be caused by the death of a relative or a beloved pet, a family move, separation from parents for extended periods, pressure to succeed, overly strict discipline, and natural disasters (even when the child has only seen them on television).

Not all stress can, or should, be avoided. Young children do not view the world as adults do. Misunderstandings or feelings of confusion can build up and leave children with stress they cannot handle alone. Young children cannot easily verbalize these feelings, so we adults must be aware of physical or behavioral changes: loss of appetite, sleep troubles, nightmares, headaches, stomachaches, or regressive behaviors such as thumbsucking.

Children often deal with stress through their play. They may act out events they find disturbing. One child may re-create an airplane crash after hearing about a real airline accident. Another may use dolls to have a conversation about divorce. This type of play helps children cope with events and feelings that might otherwise be overwhelming.

Adults play an important role in helping children cope with stress by providing a supportive atmosphere in which to talk about or play out concerns. We need to acknowledge and accept the feelings children express and give them our support, at home and at school. An attitude of love, understanding, and acceptance helps children get through difficult times.

66

Children's behavior at school is often different than it is at home. Any child can have an "off" day, but if you observe behaviors that might indicate unusual stress, be sure to tell parents about them. These conversations may not be easy to initiate, but parents need this information. It will be much easier to express your concerns if you have had several previous conversations with the parent about the more positive behaviors you've observed in their child.

The Fine Art of Daydreaming

Many adults think a child's mind and body should be continually busy. They believe that only when kids are *doing* something are they learning.

But a tendency to overschedule can actually be counterproductive to the learning process. It doesn't allow a child time to be inventive or reflective. Just as young children need periods of time for creative play, they also need time to daydream.

Daydreaming is a magical experience—anything can happen and all things are possible. The relaxed state that occurs during a daydream allows the brain to filter out distractions of the moment and to go into a creative surge of imagination and reality. Like the blending of paints, the hows, whys, and what-ifs of the daydream swirl together, forming a palette of colorful ideas.

Many a great idea begins as a daydream. Orville Wright dreamed of flying. Alexander Graham Bell dreamed of an invention to communicate over long distances. Harriet Tubman and Martin Luther King Jr. dreamed of freedom. Each held onto a dream, continued to question, and worked to make it come true.

We can help children find ways to explore their daydreams by giving them the tools to help bring the ideas into the real world. Give them time to ponder. Help them collect facts and gather materials for building and inventing. Let them choose their own methods. Help them evaluate their results. Provide opportunities to try again. Above all, we must value the questions and believe in the possibilities.

 See also: **2 86**

Children's Friendships

Children today are beginning earlier in social situations, and they are spending more time with peers than they used to. With more mothers of preschool-age children joining the work force, more children are in child care settings.

Recent studies have found that some friendships formed in the early years of childhood are second only to family relationships in importance. From such findings comes a heightened awareness of the social and emotional importance of friendships in the early years.

Enrollment in an early childhood program offers children social experiences that might not be available to them in relationships with adults or siblings. With many friends her own age, a child encounters lots of opportunities to negotiate and compromise. Children are encouraged to express opinions and ideas, as well as to respect others.

Interaction with and acceptance by peers have long-term effects on a child's life. Preschoolers develop social competence in three main areas: initiating interactions, maintaining ongoing relationships, and solving conflicts with other children.

While some children easily join a group at play, others have difficulty. As adults, we can help young children learn social strategies for entering play groups or for talking to other children about what they want. Watching for a few minutes and then saying "I'll be the sister. Okay?" works better than "Hey, let me do that!" And "That's a nice building. Would you like to build a bridge to it?" is more effective than "I want to play with the blocks, too."

We need not be too concerned when children frequently change best friends. A friendship may last only for an afternoon of play.

However, if a child does not seem to have any special friendships at school, he may benefit from one-on-one time with one of the other children outside of the early childhood setting. Playing together a few times outside of school often gives two children a level of comfort with each other that carries over to their time at school.

Early childhood educators know the value of friendships in children's lives. That's one reason we model for children appropriate, friendly behavior in social situations. Children learn appropriate social behaviors best by observing how significant adults in their lives interact with others.

Think about how you talk to the teacher in the next room. When you ask to borrow something, do you show true appreciation? When you pass others in the hallway, do you share a friendly greeting? Do you apologize when you inadvertently hurt a child's feelings?

What about the families of your students? While some parents are naturally easier to befriend than others, it is important for us to build a relationship of trust and mutual respect with all parents.

See also: **9** **73** 82

69

Share with families the ways that you make choices a regular part of your classroom practice. Explain how children are allowed to make individual choices such as where they will work, with whom, and what they will create. Describe how children as a group make choices through democratic vote, such as voting on what to have for a snack or what color of paper to use for class books.

By allowing children to make choices in the classroom and by sharing that practice with families, we help children gain more choices and help parents understand the types of choices that children should make.

Helping Children Make Decisions

Helping children learn to make decisions is challenging for parents, teachers, and caregivers. Children do not always make the wisest choices. Occasionally, however, experiencing the consequences of a poor decision is the best learning experience. It is through making small decisions that children develop the judgment and self-confidence to make larger and larger decisions as they grow older.

Clearly, children need experience in making decisions, including those that are important to them. At the same time, we should not allow young children to make decisions that might harm them or others.

Choices must be between acceptable alternatives. For example, we can invite a child to choose between wearing a green shirt or a blue shirt, having vegetable soup or a cheese sandwich for lunch, or picking up blocks or puzzles first. In these cases, either decision the child makes is a good one.

Experience and confidence from making such simple decisions gives the toddler or preschooler the basis for making bigger decisions as an older child. As we adults continue to expand the decisionmaking opportunities we offer a child, the better decision-maker he or she will become.

Aggressiveness in Children

Children who have not learned to control anger or frustration often resort to aggressive behavior. Aggression is a normal expression of emotion in young children. They have not yet learned acceptable ways to channel their anger.

Aggressive behavior includes hitting, throwing things, name-calling, spitting, biting, pushing or pulling, forcing someone to do or not do something, destroying property, and taking someone else's possessions.

Our program recognizes the importance of dealing with aggressive behavior. Teachers help children find acceptable ways to express their anger, negotiate to get what they want or need, and handle aggression directed toward them by peers.

We encourage children to express their feelings in words and to negotiate resolutions to conflict. We facilitate conversations between children when problems arise. Sometimes we even suggest words that help communicate the children's feelings. In time, with adult support, they are able to use these social skills to solve their own problems.

At home, when your child behaves aggressively, try redirecting his or her attention by offering a choice of other activities. Emphasize words rather than actions. With time and practice, a child will learn to say, "I'm mad because I want to play with the truck," instead of lashing out.

As adults, we can help children learn to express negative emotions in more appropriate ways. And a positive attitude on our part is the best teacher.

Children's aggressiveness can be a considerable issue in early childhood programs. Some parents, worried about their own child, may label other children in your program. When this happens, your efforts to help these children fit into your classroom may be undermined.

Parents who are concerned about aggressive children, either theirs or someone else's, often have exaggerated images of the extent of aggression. A visit to the classroom to observe what really happens can reassure parents that while aggressive behavior does occur, the room is far from being a constant battlefield.

As early childhood educators, we need to help parents understand aggression in the context of children's emotional development. In addition to inviting parents to observe in the classroom, you might plan a family meeting that features someone knowledgeable about children's emotional development.

See also: **66 68 71 73 77 80** 84

If you are considering using this article or the previous one ("Aggressiveness in Children") in response to a child or two in the group showing the behavior, you will need to use tact and judgment. Clearly, many parents whose children are showing a problem behavior are sensitive on the subject and may be embarrassed or affronted if they feel their child or family is being singled out. It may help to talk with the child's parents before sending such a message to all the families. You can explain that you are trying to help the other parents better understand biting (or aggression) so that they do not get overly concerned.

Of course, seeing this message in the newsletter or the child's backpack may be the first clue to many parents that an incident has occurred. This could create a wave of concern where there was none! Yet, just knowing a little more about a worrisome behavior and how the program is responding can be very reassuring and may keep parents from panicking or blaming the child or family. You will be the best judge of whether and how to use these two articles.

A Bit on Biting

Biting is a behavior that is very disturbing to all concerned. It frightens the child who is bitten and alarms his parents. It also worries the parents of the child who bites—and often scares the biter as well.

Although most children do not bite, especially after age 3, biting is by no means rare in groups of young children. When it does occur, biting cannot be ignored.

Children bite for different reasons. Sometimes they feel frustrated or threatened; in other cases, they get a sense of power over others. We try to help children recognize their feelings and learn words to express them.

We must clearly label biting as unacceptable and explain the reason in words that the child can understand. After first comforting and caring for the child who was bitten, we say something like this: "Biting hurts. I do not allow other people to hurt you and I will not allow you to hurt other people by biting them. You may not bite anyone."

If biting happens again, we may remove the child from the other children. We will explain that she can play with the others only if she does not bite.

We make it a major priority to prevent further biting, both to avoid damage to potential "bitees" and because the shrieks and tears of another child are often rewarding to the biter—increasing the chances of still more biting. Other children in the group may decide to try biting, too.

To nip biting in the bud, we assign an adult to stick close to the child who has bitten, ready to jump in and prevent a bite. Of course, we also talk with the child's parents to ensure that we're all responding consistently—at home and at school. In addition, we want to see what parents notice about the biting, such as cues that the child is about to bite or observations about situations in which biting seems to happen.

We want all parents to know that we take prompt, determined action to eliminate biting in our classroom. In the past, our methods have worked. Biting has been brought to a quick stop.

The Gift of Laughter

Humor is an important part of our everyday lives. As a form of intellectual play, it grows more sophisticated with age. The kind of humor children express depends, in part, on the level of cognitive development they have achieved.

A child first experiences humor in the second year of life in the context of playing with objects. A 3-year-old usually thinks it's hilarious to give objects or events names that she knows to be incorrect. She probably will giggle if a rabbit is called a bird. Most 4-year-olds laugh at objects primarily on the basis of their appearance. A drawing of a car with square tires, for example, might keep a boy laughing throughout the day.

Unexpected behavior also provokes laughter in young children. Seeing a grown-up jump rope or dress up in play clothes and wig can send a kid into a fit of laughter. A description of an impossible event, such as the term "It's raining cats and dogs" also can produce giggles.

Most 3- to 5-year-olds don't understand many of the jokes, riddles, or puns that seem funny to older children. Younger children do enjoy changing the words of jokes and repeating them often. For example, "Why did the chicken cross the road? . . . Because he wanted to!" can break up a child. We adults may not understand the joke, but we can appreciate the reaction it brings to our children.

Humor is more than just a chuckle or a belly laugh. It releases pent-up energy and permits the expression of ideas and feelings. Growing up is stressful, and good mental health—which includes a sense of humor—allows children to cope with sources of conflict and distress.

As early childhood educators we know the value of laughter in changing a mood, enhancing a learning situation, and building a sense of community. Families benefit from laughing together. We can help parents by providing a list of age-appropriate, humorous books. Let parents know about books that the children in the group are currently chuckling over.

See also: **66**

Sharing Is Learning

Young children have a hard time understanding the concept of sharing. They are *egocentric*—that is, they are at a stage where they view themselves as the center of the world and see the world only from their own perspective. They do not easily see the viewpoint of another person.

As parents and teachers, we sometimes mistake egocentricity for selfishness. But they are not the same. Egocentricity refers to the total inability to see another's viewpoint. It is normal in young children. Selfishness, on the other hand, is doing something for one's own benefit, knowing that it may inconvenience or even hurt someone.

Sharing is learned behavior. It is up to us to instill in our children the value of sharing. We can help kids learn to express their feelings and understand the feelings of others. At the same time, we should not shame any child for not sharing.

To foster sharing in our program, we have toys that promote cooperation, such as blocks, water center toys, and big puzzles. When two children want to play with the same toy, we try to help them work out a way that they can use it together, take turns, or reach some other solution. But it is a long process.

Most children do not begin to *decenter* until they turn 5 or 6, when they begin to see themselves in relation to other children. Even then, some traces of egocentricity remain until the child is 11 or 12. Instilling the values of sharing requires continuous support and encouragement by teachers and parents.

 See also: **21 68**

Fostering Self-Esteem

Children need to develop positive self-esteem—to feel good about who they are. Self-confidence is fostered when children have challenging activities that they can master and when adults give them real decisions and choices about their learning.

Young children gain confidence as they accomplish difficult tasks. As they work through the stages of development, new challenges and tasks present themselves every day. Confidence is built as kids learn to tie their own shoes, spell their names, or complete a puzzle.

Teachers offer activities and materials that continually challenge each child. One way we do that is through arranging different work areas in the room. In each of the areas is a variety of materials and activities. Children work in the area of their own choice and choose their own materials. Through this freedom, they begin to understand that their decisions have value.

As a parent you can be a partner in building your child's self-esteem. Giving children responsibilities at home and increasing the responsibilities with age help to build a child's self-esteem. Encouraging a child by specific comments is also effective. An acknowledgment of a job well done—for example, "I noticed you carefully folded all of your socks and put them away"—has more meaning to a child than a quick, general "Good job."

Early childhood expert Lilian Katz reminds us that esteem is conveyed to children when adults treat them with respect. We respect children when we ask them for their views and preferences and when we provide opportunities for real decisions and choices about those things that matter to them.

See also: **5 69 77 91–92**

Family Matters

The following group of articles addresses many of the questions and concerns that families have. These short articles cannot replace face-to-face conversations. However, they can be used to reinforce or augment sound, logical advice about parenting.

Parents may turn to us for advice about problems they are having with their child or about decisions they are about to make concerning their child. We are experts in their eyes. We have training in child development and probably have more access to research concerning parenting and child growth and development. Because of this, it is vital that we, as teachers or directors, help families make good decisions for their children. These articles can be used to reinforce discussions that directors and teachers have with parents or to introduce a topic.

75

A strong home/school connection is essential when building a good environment for young children. As teachers and directors, we must initiate and develop this relationship.

It is up to us to make families feel welcome. We should make clear to parents that they are welcome at any time. Parents are often wary of intruding in the classroom and do not want to offend us by their presence or questions. Be honest with parents and let them know that while the children are our first priority, we also want to spend time talking with them. We can recommend times when our programs are best suited for informal conversations—perhaps at drop-off, pickup, or by telephone. To ensure that a strong bridge is built between home and school, we must help parents feel relaxed and welcome. We must nurture mutual trust and respect at every opportunity.

Bridging Home and School

We all know that if a bridge is not structurally sound, it will eventually collapse. Likewise, if relationships are not built on a sturdy foundation, they too will fail.

Too often parents and program staff are intimidated by each other. But by willingly beginning the home/school relationship with an open, sharing approach, we can build trust. Then, when issues arise—even sticky ones—we can talk about them without hesitation.

All of us here try to do our best to keep you informed. We post pertinent information on the parent bulletin board as well as include it in the newsletter. We send home other information with your child. We also want to talk with each of you often.

Feel welcome to visit the classroom at any time. Come eat lunch with us. Drop by and tell us a story or show us something special. Or just take a break, have a seat, and enjoy the children.

Clearly, ongoing interaction and support from both families and staff make the connection between home and school a two-way street. You can help by sharing information about your child with us. Especially during any crisis or period of change, when children are under stress and act or react differently, please keep us informed. Obvious times include a change in jobs, a move to a new house, or an illness or death in the family, but they also could involve the child experiencing nightmares, making changes in eating habits, and stopping or starting medication. Of course, anything you share with a member of our staff will be held in confidence.

In turn, we'll alert you to anything out of the ordinary that we might notice in your child here at the center. Only by sharing information can we build a bridge strong enough to support our children.

 See also: 9 65

What Did You Do at School Today?

It is difficult for young children to recall and describe what they did during the program day. Children are active and busy for the entire time, but they sometimes lack the words to tell others about their activities—or by the time you pick them up, they have moved on to other things.

Parents, of course, want to know about their child's day. Here are a few ideas to keep in mind when asking your child about his or her activities.

- Keep informed of the class's planned events so you can ask specific questions. For example, "Did you get to go on the nature walk today, or was it too rainy?"

- With most children, avoid general questions like "What happened at school today?"

- Avoid questions that produce one-word answers.

- Ask specific questions such as
  — "Whose 'sharing time' was it today? Tell me about what she/he shared."
  — "What was in the art center today?"
  — "Tell me about this drawing in your backpack."

Sometimes telling the child a little something about your own day starts the ball rolling. The child may get the idea of sharing news and feelings about his or her day.

Newsletter articles or letters sent home about upcoming events are very effective in sharing specific information about what is going on in class. Among other things, this information helps families communicate with their child and ask specific questions. Here's an example.

The 4-year-olds will have a visit from Mr. Insect Guy on April 4th. Mr. Insect Guy will bring a collection of insects that he has collected from all over the world. He has giant beetles and beautiful butterflies.

With this type of information a family member can ask a child specific questions about Mr. Insect Guy and his visit. Parents are informed, and the connection between home and school is strengthened.

To help keep parents aware of what's happening in the program and to give them conversation openers, some teachers leave brief messages on families' answering machines, voice mail, or e-mail. For example, say, "Ask Tony about the giant moth" or "Ask Sheila what monkeys eat." Sometimes your information tidbits can build on what a particular child did. If Khalid helped make an impressive block building that day, for instance, his parents would love to know about it.

See also: 8 75

Discipline is one issue that concerns every parent—and every teacher. Some parents have definite ideas about parenting, while others are still searching for answers. As teachers, each of us has struggled with managing a difficult child. We know how exasperating it can be, and many times we do not have the answers.

Many parents will find the hints in this message very familiar (although carrying them out consistently is another matter). If your group of parents is mostly of that mind, tailor the article to be more of a reminder, sort of a parenting primer that we all know but need to remind ourselves of. With parents who discipline very differently, more explanation or examples might be needed.

Consider a parents-only meeting to discuss discipline. Arrange to provide care for the children during the session, so parents will feel free to ask specific questions about their child.

You might invite a parenting expert to lead the discussion and answer questions. Be prepared with information on local parenting classes and groups, including inexpensive or free services, especially if your program serves low-income families. If parents express strong interest in participating in a parenting group, you might consider having one at the center.

It is important that all the adults in a child's life are as consistent as possible in the guidance approach that they use. At the parents' meeting, share the methods—and even the language—that you use with children. Give examples of phrases you use and set up scenarios to illustrate the examples. Explain why you do what you do.

In conferences with individual families, discuss parents' goals for their child's self-control and the techniques and consequences they use at home for inappropriate behavior.

93 | *See also:* **70 78** |

Helping Children Develop Self-Discipline

Children's misbehavior can be frustrating and disturbing to adults, but we also can see it as an opportunity to teach, a chance to model self-discipline and character. Emotional development, like other learning, takes time and learning opportunities. And children, being the excellent imitators they are, will follow our example—for better or worse.

If we yell at children, they will yell; if we hit them, they will hit. Or they will become the perpetual victims of others' aggression. We get better results when we discipline calmly and teach our children to express their feelings in acceptable ways. When teachers share, children share; when parents are courteous, children are more cooperative.

Here are a few things we do in the classroom; they also work for parents.

Be clear and consistent. Set and discuss rules and consequences. Rules should be clear, simple, and few. Some adults have only one basic rule: *You may not hurt yourself, others, or things.* For example, to stop a child from hitting another child, kneel and calmly state, "You may not hit Ben. People are not for hitting." Then add, "I know you are angry. Can you tell me why? . . . OK, how can you let Ben know that you want to use the blue crayon?"

Offer choices. "Do you want to brush your teeth now, or do you want to brush after we read a story?" "Would you like milk or juice with your snack?"

Ignore certain behavior, like cursing or stomping, if it is not harmful. A child will quickly learn that he will gain nothing by acting up. On the other hand, he will learn that good behavior gets results and a favorable reaction from grown-ups.

No matter what we adults do, there are times when children lose control. Aggressive acts may call for removing the child from the action in a brief time-out. However, a time-out period may backfire if used in the spirit of punishment ("Go to your room right now!"). The point is to give the child a few minutes to cool down. Those minutes come in handy, too, for helping a frustrated parent or teacher cool down—and think of what to do next!

Minimizing Power Struggles

No matter how compliant a child, there will be times when he does not want to put on his socks or when she refuses to pick up her toys. As young children develop, they begin to understand that they can make their own decisions. And occasionally they make a power play at an inconvenient time.

While a power play can be frustrating for the adult who is trying to get the child to do something, it is a healthy part of children's social/emotional development. These incidents help children develop a stronger sense of self and the capability to set their own limits.

We adults need to react appropriately. In many instances, trying to force the child to do what he has said he will not do escalates the situation into a full-blown power struggle.

Try offering assistance instead. For example, you might say, "You can put on your socks by yourself or I can help you this morning." Or, "I could help you put away your toys. Would you like that?"

Or offer choices. "OK, you don't want to wear these socks today. Would you rather wear blue ones or green ones?" "Let's see. Which would it be easier to start with: putting the blocks in this tub or putting the cars back in their case?"

Power plays are simply a part of growing up. When handled by adults in a calm manner, they offer opportunities for children to develop self-esteem and self-control.

See also: **69 77 84** 94

79

Consider having a family meeting designed to highlight problem solving. After welcoming the families, divide the adults into several work groups and give them a problem to solve. Here's a possibility.

Each group is to measure the room, using any materials that are available. Parents do not have to use standard units of measure but can if they wish. They should decide as a group how they will measure the room.

After measuring and recording their findings, parents are to draw a large diagram that depicts their measurements and shows the location of all permanent fixtures. As the groups begin to work, walk around and record some of the skills being used during this exercise—math skills such as estimating, adding, and multiplying, and social skills such as negotiating. Allow the groups 20 minutes or so to work on the task.

Have the groups share their findings and post their sketches. Now have the participants tell you what skills they used during this activity. List these on an overhead or chart paper. Point out the things that you wrote down during your observations if these have not been mentioned.

Explain that this kind of involvement and discovery is the way young children learn best. Leaving the activity open-ended allows children to try out ideas, see what works, make decisions, negotiate with their friends, and solve problems. The teacher serves as facilitator and helps the children succeed by supplying additional materials or helping them approach a solution.

Parents can return to their groups and brainstorm the skills a child might use to solve similar everyday problems, such as conflict over the use of blocks, deciding how to fairly divide a bag of pretzels, and determining a procedure for putting water in the water table.

Solving Problems

Problem-solving skills develop through repeated practice. Problems exist all around us, but all too often, adults solve children's problems without realizing that we are missing opportunities for children to learn how to solve their own problems.

For example, suppose your family is about to sit down for a meal and there aren't enough clean forks for everyone. The typical adult solution to this problem is to quickly wash a few forks. But that is not the only solution. You could use plastic forks. You could eat with spoons that night. Or you could use chopsticks.

Generating solutions with a child may take a little longer than just solving the problem yourself. But thinking through simple family problems together strengthens the child's problem-solving skills, including use of these four steps:

- identifying the problem,
- brainstorming possible solutions,
- choosing one solution and trying it out, and
- evaluating what happened.

Look for simple, everyday problems that might intrigue your child. Her critical skills will sharpen with use, and she may come up with solutions you never imagined.

Keeping Superheroes in Check

Television and movie themes feature many superheroes who are irresistible to children. In these stories there is a stark distinction between good and evil characters, and it seems that they always resort to fighting to settle problems.

Parents have to decide how to respond to this kind of programming. As you sort through your feelings, you should realize that children probably will invent good and evil characters, even without the influence of the Ninja Turtles or the Power Rangers. Remember, long before television, children played cops and robbers, Robin Hood and the sheriff, and the like.

The impact of superheroes depends a lot on how much time children spend watching television and videos. Viewing one half-hour program a week may have little effect on a child, but three hours is another matter. If you watch programs with your child and talk about the characters and their actions, you can help keep superhero tactics in perspective.

You also may find it helpful to read about peaceful real-life heroes like Martin Luther King Jr., Helen Keller, and Johnny Appleseed. Talk about their courage and determination and how they overcame obstacles without resorting to violence.

When children play superheroes, keep an eye on their play to make sure aggression does not get out of hand. Whatever your family decides about superhero play, you should communicate with your child how you feel about violence and how to stand up for beliefs.

With careful adult guidance and lots of discussion, children can understand the difference between superhero fantasy battles against the bad guys and how we ordinary human beings deal with the evils we encounter in the real world.

Not all parents are of one mind regarding violent themes in children's play, televised violence, and related issues. While some parents strongly oppose aggressive play and violent programming, others own guns, buy their kids toy guns, and allow them to watch TV programs, movies, and videos with lots of violent action.

Your program may adopt policies or practices—such as no gun play at school—that differ from parents' preferences, and it is legitimate to do so. However, you need to help parents understand the reasons for your decisions, and you cannot do this effectively without knowing the range of opinions and reactions among the participating families. Before shaping your newsletter message or other communication with families about such issues, find out what parents in your program think. Take care to treat their views respectfully in all your communications.

With respect to media violence, you can reach parents who are inclined to worry about its effects on kids and parents who dismiss the idea—and, of course, you may have both types in your program—by suggesting alternatives for children's viewing. Provide a listing of children's TV shows, videos, and/or movies, perhaps including parents' suggestions based on what their children have enjoyed. Information on quality programming and videos is also available from sources such as the National Foundation to Improve Television (60 State St., Boston, MA 02109; 617-523-6353); the Coalition for Quality Children's Video, which publishes a directory of quality children's videos (535 Cordova Rd., Suite 456, Sante Fe, NM 87501; 505-989-8076); and the Children's Video Report, which reviews video materials for preschool and elementary-school children.

Consider using the superhero article in conjunction with a local or national event such as National TV Turn-Off Week and including activities for families to enjoy instead of TV, again perhaps solicited through the newsletter. Then, during the no-TV period, you might invite parents to keep a notebook of observations, kid quotes, and children's drawings, which can be shared through a bulletin board or newsletter.

See also: **10   27   70**

Games similar to I Spy are played in many cultures but under different names. Along with this article, it would be helpful to include the rules for I Spy. Here's a brief version.

Two or more people can play I Spy. A "spyer" chooses an item to describe (in a car or bus, choices should be limited to items inside the vehicle because outside objects move past too quickly). He or she says, "I spy something that is (a color, a shape, or a relative size)." The first guesser makes a guess and, if wrong, the second guesser tries, and so on. Then the spyer gives another clue, and a new round of guesses starts. The game continues until the object is identified or the players give up.

On the Road Again

Have you ever thought about how much time you and your child spend in transit each day? Whether you drive a car, pedal a bicycle, take a bus or subway, or walk, you and your child are together during that time. With a little planning, your journeys can become shared moments of fun and learning.

Before you go to the store, for example, involve your child in making a shopping list. You can ask your child to check the cereal boxes to see if any are almost empty. A 4- or 5-year-old also can check on the supply of milk, extra rolls of toilet tissue, and other items. Later, you can consult this list together as you shop.

As you proceed on your errands, read signs around you. Take along paper and pencil for mapping out your stops. Help orient your child by pointing out stores and streets you pass along the way.

After a busy day at school, your child may need a break from the hustle of the schedule. Bring along a light snack or something cool to drink for the trip home. (Some items such as lollipops are not safe in the car or on the bus; choose snacks with care.) Usually it's a good idea to take a little quiet break before you begin discussing the day's events or focusing on the next stop.

On days when neither of you feels like talking, a couple of sing-along or storybook tapes, kept in an activity bag or backpack, will come in handy. Drawing materials, large dice, card games, small toys, puzzles, and books make great additions to a backpack.

Before a long trip, gather information and read about the destination to help your child look forward to the excursion. Together, map out points of interest along the way.

Games like I Spy, searching for animals, counting colored cars, matching sign shapes, finding silly-named streets, looking for out-of-state license plates, or inventing rhymes amuse away the miles.

When your child's attention begins to wander, switch to another game or take a break. Plan frequent stretch-and-bend stops to satisfy the wiggles. And don't forget that favorite pillow or stuffed animal!

Children and Pets

Most children love animals, whether they are watching lions and gorillas at the zoo, romping with the family dog, or feeding the classroom guinea pig. This natural attraction is the perfect opportunity for children to learn some basic concepts about the animal world and to care for something other than themselves.

Pets—like people—have basic needs: a safe place to live, the right foods to eat, and water to drink. Each animal, however, has specific housing and food needs. Even young children can learn that rodents must chew on hard foods to keep their teeth from growing too long, that fish must have clean water to breathe, or that turtles require a variety of fruits, vegetables, and meat. They can learn that parakeets depend on people to keep their cages clean and that housecats need frequent litter-box changes.

Children also learn that different animals must be handled in different ways. They learn to be gentle with small animals, and they realize that they must help some pets get exercise.

Some families are not allowed to have cats and dogs in the apartment or house that they rent. Small animals that live in aquariums or cages, such as fish, hermit crabs, or hamsters, make ideal pets in these situations.

Other families choose not to own pets because of allergies or preference. Children in these families may learn at school about caring for live animals. Some kids even pretend to care for stuffed-animal pets at home.

Whatever children's particular experiences with pets, these enhance kids' sense of responsibility and caring.

Children's drawings of their pets or a pet they would like to have could be used in your newsletter with this article. Children also could describe their pet or tell what it likes. These descriptions make nice highlights for the article or captions for the drawings.

After reading this article in your newsletter, parents might want further information about what animals make the most suitable pets for young children. You could ask people at a local pet shop to provide a list of kid-friendly pets and the factors that families need to consider with each kind of pet.

Perhaps someone at the pet shop or a parent who has experience with animals would volunteer to talk to the children and provide tips on caring for common pets, especially cats and dogs. Also helpful would be a list of alternative pets for families that have constraints such as someone with allergies or a no-pets-allowed lease.

See also: **62–63**

Periodically include recipes for nutritional snacks, review a children's cookbook, or give examples of balanced menus that children find tempting and parents find easy. Invite families to share simple recipes for dishes from their traditional cultures.

But I Hate Broccoli!

Parents often worry because they think their young children don't eat enough. Some children seem to be naturally finicky. But others simply may be so overwhelmed by the amount of food placed on their plates that they don't know where or how to begin eating.

How much food is enough? And how can we get our children to participate more successfully in mealtimes?

Physicians tell us that a child needs one tablespoon of food per year of age at each meal. That means a 3-year-old needs at least three tablespoons of food at breakfast, at lunch, and at dinner in order to maintain health and growth. These are not the heaping portions that we are tempted to put on our children's plates; they are standard measurement portions.

Allowing children to serve themselves encourages them to eat larger portions of a variety of foods. When children get to control their choices and the amount of food they take, mealtime becomes more enjoyable for them and you. Participation in meal planning and preparation also encourages children to feel that they are a part of the process of mealtime.

A family meal can be a time of conversation and relaxation or a time of frustration and anger. By offering children smaller amounts, the opportunity to help prepare meals, and the chance to serve themselves, we can provide a calmer, more satisfying family time for everyone.

Family Routines

Children develop best in an environment of order and consistency. They are happier when they know what to expect. To a young child, a predictable world is a safe world.

By setting up regular, reliable times and procedures for daily events, parents and teachers provide a dependable environment. Routines also help avoid the power struggles that so often occur between adults and children.

You'll find life with your child goes more smoothly if you set up and consistently carry out regular routines such as bedtime, wake-up time, mealtimes, chore times, play times, and homework times. It might help to have a list of the sequence of daily events posted where your child can refer to it as necessary (for example, Bedtime—put on pajamas, brush teeth, read story). Use simple drawings on the schedule to facilitate young children's understanding (kids love to help with such drawings).

Of course, some changes in schedules and routines are unavoidable. And while children prefer routine, they are resilient enough when a familiar routine has to be disturbed.

There are two basic points to remember:

Be consistent. Children are the most content when the same thing happens at pretty much the same time every day; and

Explain deviations from the routine. If you have to change your plans, let your child know ahead of time, if possible, and explain the situation and the change you are making.

See also: **78**

Keep aware of temporary exhibits at local or nearby museums and scan newspaper entertainment sections that list current museum exhibits. In the newsletter run brief notices of exhibits and events that are of particular interest to young children. Also remind families of any local activities that would make ideal weekend outings.

Try to assemble a set of prints that families can borrow. You might organize them by artist, medium, subject, or genre (still lifes, portraits, landscapes, and so forth).

Since some families are intimidated by art museums and might not visit without your encouragement, you might want to plan a family field trip to a museum. Interested families could meet you there.

Prepare handouts that highlight a few particular pieces of art so families will have some common information to use as a springboard for discussion. Encourage everyone to talk about paintings, photographs, and sculptures they like.

Visiting Art Museums

The quiet atmosphere of art museums and the exuberance of young children may seem to be at odds with each other. But with some advance planning, art museums can be a wonderful place for young children.

Before you go to an art museum or gallery with your child, talk about the behavior that is expected inside: walking and talking quietly and looking without touching. At first, keep museum visits short, taking the lead from your child on how long is long enough.

One way to help young children feel comfortable about the museum visit is to turn the trip into an art adventure. As you enter the museum, go first to the gift shop and sort through the postcards together. Let your child choose her favorite painting or sculpture (checking first with the clerk to make sure the piece of artwork is on display, not just in the museum's collection). Postcards are inexpensive, but the artwork that is illustrated can become the child's special piece of art to look for as she goes through the museum.

Enjoy this time with your child. Share what you notice, what you like and don't like. Go at your child's pace and follow where her interest takes you. You'll see things you never saw before.

Too Much of a Good Thing

A minivan weaves through afternoon traffic. Its bumper sticker proclaims "Mom's Taxi."

A generation ago few children had as much organized activity in their lives as they do today. Most days consisted of attending school, playing in the yard or neighborhood, eating the evening meal, and preparing for school the next day. Some young children had a piano lesson, baseball practice, or a ballet class one afternoon a week, but few encountered today's great variety of programming options.

While extracurricular activities can provide children an opportunity to learn important skills, some families today overdo it. Some kids have not just one extracurricular activity a week, but maybe two a day! Some are involved in sports every season and also enrolled in dance class, music lessons, karate instruction, swimming lessons, and more.

These activities are also beginning at an earlier age. It's not uncommon to hear 3-year-olds discussing their busy schedules.

Some children excel at such activities, but too much programming can have detrimental effects. It's stressful to be rushed from one activity to the next. It is tiring to be in an organized program all day, or even for several hours, and then be taken to another class in the evening. Kids need time to play and relax in whatever ways they want. Also, the reduction of contact with family and close friends is a loss for young children.

We should ask ourselves several questions if we suspect overprogramming. *Is this activity good for my child's self-esteem? Is this something she is interested in and enjoys? Is he overly tired? Has she begun to exhibit behavior problems not previously present?* If the answer to any of these questions is yes, it may be time to rethink the extracurricular schedule.

86 *Our society has a tendency to push young children into activities that they may not be ready for. When you use this article in your newsletter, you might include a list of books and articles (see the Resources section) that deal with this issue. Many books give further evidence of the damage that may be done to our children if we, as the adults in their lives, allow them to be rushed and pushed into too many activities.*

See also: **5 66 87**

87

Organized sports and activities are often inappropriate, and even unsafe, for young children. If parents are in doubt about enrolling their child in team sports or signing up for lessons in ballet, tumbling, tap, or karate, you might suggest that they consult their family physician. You also can recommend some books listed in the Resources section. Better yet, keep photocopies of articles that deal with early involvement in team sports.

The development of teamwork, which is one of the things parents seek in organized sports, can be promoted in other ways. Nothing builds a sense of community among families and staff like working together. Families, children, and teachers can tackle jobs such as sprucing up the playground, giving the classroom a thorough cleaning, painting a mural in the hallway, or preparing a Thanksgiving feast. Such activities mix the practical with the playful.

Projects to benefit the community—cleaning up the park, setting up a "victory garden," planting flowers at a nursing home, launching a toy drive—also underline the concept of teamwork. In addition, they show children that parents and teachers value helping others and working for the good of the community.

On special workdays, list some phrases of encouragement (*We couldn't have done it without you! We make a good team, don't we? Everyone sure is doing their part* and the like) so parents can use them throughout the day—and carry them home. During breaks, play games that emphasize team participation, not winning.

Is It Too Soon for Organized Sports?

If you've ever watched a group of 4- or 5-year-olds playing soccer or teeball, you've probably seen a player or two stray away to pick flowers, do somersaults, or watch a plane pass overhead. Such behavior is typical for children of this age, who usually are not yet ready for organized sports.

Somewhere between the ages of 6 and 7, most children develop the mental capacity to understand rules and focus on the game for more than a few minutes. They become more capable of working together as a team and gain the maturity necessary to deal with defeat. But prior to this point in development, most young children are just not ready to play an organized sport.

Pediatricians also have concerns about sports injuries to children. Ask your child's doctor about the risks of a specific sport and whether your child is physically ready to play.

Give some thought to your child's emotional development as well. Children vary widely in personality and emotional maturity, and you know your child better than anyone. Involvement in organized sports before the child is developmentally ready can hurt his self-esteem and self-confidence. Waiting a few years allows him time to develop the physical, mental, and emotional capacities necessary to play team sports.

Meanwhile, many activities at school and at home lay the groundwork for team play. Here at school we frequently plan cooperative activities and projects where children work together, such as preparing a meal, making a mural, or designing a block city.

At home, you can make a point of involving your children in tasks where cooperation is key, even simple two-person jobs like folding a sheet or using a dustpan. When kids hear "Good teamwork, guys!" or "We finished so quickly because everyone helped!" they see the value of working together. This will stand them in good stead when it's time for team sports.

 See also: **22–23 66 86**

Choosing Software for Children

Computers are a terrific learning tool, even in preschool, if used in ways that are appropriate for young children. When choosing software for the center, we apply criteria developed by two experts (Dan Shade and Susan Haughland) on computer use with young children. We'd like to share these criteria with you as you look for software for your child to use at home.

When considering software, ask yourself: Is it

age appropriate for the child? The software should provide realistic expectations for young children. The subject should be interesting and involve the child in an active way—not just in drill and practice.

designed to give the child control? The child is an active participant, initiating and deciding the sequence of events rather than simply doing tasks that have one right answer.

easy for the child to understand? For children who are not yet readers, instructions should be given by the computer's synthesized speech function or feature a picture menu.

relatively easy for the child to use alone? Good software for young children should function smoothly with a minimal amount of adult supervision.

Before you use this article in a newsletter or as a handout, think about the family demographics. Do not use the piece at all if you think most of the families do not own home computers (a beginning-of-the-year survey is an invaluable tool for finding out such things). Instead, prepare another handout that tells parents where they and their children can have access to computers (check local libraries, community centers, and the like) and emphasize the value of learning computer skills.

However, with a group of families who do own computers, consider getting parents' input on software recommendations. Include a brief notice along with this article, asking parents to use the stated criteria to rate children's software that they have at home. Encourage them to share children's comments and experiences.

Include excerpts of the comments or lists of recommended software in the next newsletter.

See also: **24**

89 ▶

A family scavenger hunt based on a nature-related theme could be launched over a weekend or even over a period of a week or two. Each child could be assigned to find with his or her family two or three items, or children could be asked to describe and draw their observations.

Of course, you'll have to tailor the hunt to your environment—urban, rural, or suburban, as well as region and season. Be creative and make the hunt an educational adventure not only for the child, but also for parents and other family members.

When all the items are gathered, the children could put together an exhibit. Parents would be invited to visit at their convenience.

Or plan a family field trip to a nature setting (botanical gardens, nature center, state park, and other such places). Families could meet at the point of destination. Invite along a naturalist or an amateur naturalist to help identify and interpret the flora and fauna.

Beauty in Nature

Natural beauty can be seen everywhere. White fluffy clouds float above the playground, a spider's web flutters in a gentle wind, the moon sometimes graces the day sky, and flowers shoot up in a nearby garden.

Short nature walks give children a chance to observe the wonders of our natural world. At school, we plan nature walks to listen for environmental sounds or to look for insects. We also take advantage of everyday opportunities such as exploring puddles after a rain shower, capturing snowflakes during the first snowfall, or playing with streamers outside during a strong wind.

Catching fireflies, smelling honeysuckle, or tossing stones into a creek can be aesthetic, relaxing experiences for kids and adults alike. Noticing nature's wonders helps children become more observant and respectful of the world around them, helps build their vocabulary as they hear adults describe what they see, and encourages drawing and painting to document their observations.

From time to time, draw children's attention to things they may not notice. Point out different rocks. Collect leaves of various kinds. Discuss the similarities and differences in flowers. (Children may be tempted to pick flowers, but be careful that they take only common ones—not rare species.) Talk about what the squirrel eats or where the robin lives. Enjoy the changes of the seasons together.

Parents can further stimulate a child's interest—say, in stars or snakes—through library visits. Field guides are available on a wide range of subjects (insects, wildflowers, mammals, trees, and so forth).

Keep specimens, drawings, magazine pictures, photos, stickers, and summaries of your child's special experiences in a scrapbook. A theme may be carried throughout the book, but young naturalists should be allowed to put in anything that strikes their fancy.

One discovery leads to another. We adults have much to learn from the natural curiosity of children.

Family Vacations

Vacations are an opportunity to build a sense of family togetherness without the pressures of everyday life. Where the family goes and how long the stay are not important, but the best vacations are planned around the interests and the developmental levels of children.

When planning a trip with young children, remember that they need and like routine. A family should keep naptime, mealtimes, and bedtimes as close to the normal routine as possible. It also helps when the itinerary is discussed so that kids know what to expect.

The family that travels with preschoolers should consider this age group's self-centeredness, short attention span, and need for movement. Children at age 3 or 4 make good travelers, though. They enjoy physical activity, quiet playtime, arts and crafts, and most of what parents suggest. They also enjoy exploring and talking about their observations and experiences.

Traveling with this age group does present some challenges. A survival kit helps minimize irritability and crankiness during long hours of driving. Pack healthy snacks, storybooks, crayons, markers, paper, games, and a tape player and tapes.

By preplanning your vacation, ensuring some routine, yet allowing for flexibility, everyone in your family can enjoy the adventure.

Give some thought to the families you serve before you run this article in a newsletter. After all, not every family can afford to take a vacation. You might want to reframe the article around outings rather than vacations. Suggest some local, inexpensive adventures. Many of the dos and don'ts in the article apply anytime the family takes a long drive and children are out of their usual routine.

See also: **81 84**

91

Teachers and classmates can help celebrate the new big-sister or big-brother status of a child. Special cards drawn and written or dictated by the children can congratulate the child and family members. The child can share photographs of the baby, as well as feelings about the new arrival. Peers then can talk about their experiences with the birth of a sibling.

Sometimes a teacher just needs to listen to a child. A few minutes of undivided attention may be just what the child needs.

Birth of a Sibling

No matter how welcome babies are, newborns cause stress in households. Parents are usually very tired. Routines change. Older children may have trouble adjusting to the new role in their expanded family.

Parents can affect the relationship between children by what they do before and after the birth. In the last several months of the pregnancy, talk with your child about the impending birth and how everybody will need to help out with the baby. Answer questions about birth, show the child pictures of himself or herself just after birth, and read books about the arrival of a sibling. Children can accompany mother to the doctor's office for prenatal checkups and visit the hospital where the birth will take place.

Prepare grandparents and other family and friends, too. When people are always asking "How's the baby?" the older child feels left out. The special adults in a child's life could be encouraged to pay special attention to the older child, inquiring about her activities and interests.

After the birth, arrange a hospital visit so the preschooler can see Mother and baby. Photograph or videotape the meeting. Consider giving the child a gift to celebrate the new role as big sister/brother—as well as a picture of the baby to take to school.

Minimize changes in the child's life by keeping up with school attendance, maintaining bathtime and bedtime routines, and trying to initiate as many conversations and playtimes as before the birth of the baby. Enlist children's help in caring for the new baby.

Changes will occur. But careful attention to family routines and observation of how children are responding can help smooth this time of transition.

Separation and Divorce

Children are greatly affected by their parents' decisions and actions. This is true in everyday life and especially so in a situation as life-altering as divorce.

Here are a few suggestions for helping a child through the trauma of separation or divorce.

- Speak to them about the separation or divorce as honestly as possible.

- Assure them that the divorce is a result of parental problems and that they did not cause the separation.

- Answer their questions to help satisfy curiosity and ease confusion and frustration.

- Listen attentively as kids share their feelings and concerns about the situation.

- Encourage expression of feelings in a variety of ways—through writing, talking, dancing, or drawing.

- Read stories together about divorce and divorced families. Ask a children's librarian to recommend books that are appropriate for your child's age and situation.

- Try to maintain family routines and continuity as much as possible, making sure that the child sees both parents on a frequent and regular basis.

Divorce is a time of difficult transition for everyone. But by being open and honest, by continuing family life as normally as possible, and by placing the best interests of their children first, parents can help kids adjust during this difficult time.

Early childhood educators have the unique joy—and stress—of caring for young children and their families. At no time is stress more evident than during a divorce. While it is not our role to counsel, advise, or evaluate the parents' situation, extra understanding and compassion on our part, as well as increased communication with parent and child, are essential.

For many mothers, divorce means reentry into the workplace or an increase in work responsibilities. Along with this often comes guilt at the lack of time spent with her child(ren) and increased financial and time constraints. Letting her know you understand is important.

For some fathers, divorce brings their first exposure to the early childhood classroom environment. They find themselves lost in a world known only by their ex-wives. It is important that teachers and directors be open and willing to help the father learn how to relate to his child's school experiences.

To both mother and father, emphasize the positive things that you hear and observe the child doing. This may help keep the focus on the positive and allow the family to realize that, in time, adjustments will occur.

See also: **66 74 77 84**

93

Families new to a city must locate many important places and services. They must find a nearby grocery store, the closest post office and library, a doctor and dentist—the list goes on. You can help by providing an inventory of "kid-friendly" places in your community. The list might include libraries with children's storytimes, museums or zoos with good children's programs, family restaurants, bookstores with outstanding children's sections, even hair stylists who are especially good with children.

As a getting-to-know-you gift for a new family in the program, ask other families to write down their favorite place for children. This helpful gesture also might start some valuable friendships.

Don't forget children and families who are leaving the program. We-will-miss-you ideas include children writing or drawing their favorite things at school or designing and signing a goodbye note. Assemble these in a class book to give to the child who is moving. Discuss with the other children their feelings about losing a friend.

Moving and Young Children

Whether a family moves a few blocks or thousands of miles, relocating is stressful for everyone, especially children. Stress-related behaviors such as aggression, loss of appetite, regression to less mature behaviors, depression, and withdrawal are not uncommon in children experiencing a move.

Adults can do much to ease the stress of moving for young children. Before the move, parents can model positive attitudes. Children are quick to mirror the emotions of people important to them. If they sense that their parents are worried, they will dread the move. But if children sense that family members are enthusiastic, they will see the move as an exciting—perhaps even promising—event.

Kids should be included in planning whenever possible. Although many decisions made during a move are not appropriate for children, house-hunting excursions or walks around a new neighborhood help them retain a sense of control during this period of change.

If a visit before the move is not possible, show the child photographs or videotapes of the new house—don't forget his or her room!—and neighborhood. Ease the fear of the unknown as much as possible. Encourage your child to participate in the many choices that have to be made in the packing process. And allow time for goodbyes in the old neighborhood.

After the move, as your kids begin to make new friends, observe the strategies they use. Children often find that strategies that worked in the old environment don't work with peers they do not know. They may need help in joining neighborhood games or groups at school. Adults can provide this assistance through modeling and role-playing.

Moving is a process rather than a single event in children's lives. And their needs differ at various times during the process. Our attention, understanding, and interaction can ease stress and facilitate children's adjustment to a new environment.

 See also: **65–66 68 84**

Communicating with Families—
The Written Word and Beyond

We decided to write this book out of our conviction that no early childhood program is effective without a high level of communication, trust, and respect between staff and parents. Parents are the foremost experts on their own children, and they have boundless love for their daughters and sons. We are eager for them to share with us what they know about their children. We want to know what their child's life is like outside the classroom and what they as parents care about.

As early childhood educators, we are experts, too. We have knowledge and understanding about child development, as well as years of experience working with children. We have reasons for what we do in our classrooms, although we often take them for granted because the fundamentals of our practice have become second nature to us. We may forget that most parents do not have this in-depth understanding of children's development and learning and that they do not know why we do things the way we do. It is our responsibility to let parents know not only *what* we do in the early childhood program but also *why*.

For it is parents who are the constant in their children's lives—they educate and guide their children from infancy through adolescence and even beyond. If we can deepen parents' understanding of their children's learning and development and their own role in it, we multiply our contribution to the child and family far beyond the impact we have in the classroom. We also contribute to parents becoming knowledgeable consumers of high-quality early childhood education.

So little time

Realizing the importance of communication with parents does not make the task easy. It is hard for busy teachers and child care directors to find the time to research and write even a simple article or handout on a topic. This book was written for that reason: to provide early childhood educators a resource for generating effective, "family-friendly communication."

Letters or newsletters for parents can include descriptions of the children's activities, samples of their work, plans for upcoming events, suggestions for activities parents can do with their children, games to play at home, words to songs and fingerplays that children are learning, recipes used in cooking activities, and other information that parents find interesting and helpful. Newsletters can be supplemented with copies of articles from professional publications and parenting magazines.

Teachers can also use displays of children's work and photographs of kids at work to convey how children benefit from the various learning centers, what they are doing in a particular project, and how key curriculum goals are achieved. Parents are drawn to photos of their children (and samples of kids' work) and accompanying descriptions can communicate a lot—how an activity intrigued and delighted the children, the skills and understandings acquired through the activity, and what a child said.

Interaction with families

Strictly speaking, newsletters and other messages to parents are teacher-to-parent (as opposed to parent-to-teacher) communication, although they do a great deal to encourage interaction and parent input. You can express your interest in parent questions and comments by sending home a note inviting family members to jot down questions or comments on an attached sheet (or stapled-together sheets), which go back and forth in a pocket folder in the child's backpack. The few moments it takes to jot down a response to a question or to thank a parent for sharing a story help build relationship with the family.

Still, there's no substitute for face-to-face interaction. Even a brief moment when the parent drops off or picks up the child can be turned into a sharing moment. Telling a story about something a child has said or done lets the parents know that you pay close attention to their child. If you think ahead and have the child's drawing or words to share with parents from time to time, you not only brighten their day; you also give them a vivid glimpse into what is going on in the classroom and an understanding of its value for the child. This kind of information sharing also takes place, of course, in parent-teacher conferences, which should be planned several times over the course of the year, as well as at other times by request of parents with a special concern.

Another familiar vehicle for communication between teachers and parents—and an important one—is the family meeting (planned for a time reasonably convenient for parents, and producing noticeably better attendance when child care is provided!). Such gatherings give staff and parents a chance to talk directly to one another. With everyone assembled in the classroom, it is easy to discuss why the room is arranged as it is, why certain activities are planned, and what children are learning in these centers and activities. Periodic family meetings help parents feel more comfortable with the teacher and with the early childhood program. If they feel comfortable, they are more likely to ask questions; if their questions about the program are answered, they are more likely to be supportive.

Children benefit when experiences at school are supported and extended at home. Sharing information in newsletters and other written messages, planning conferences and meetings with families, and answering parents' questions as they arise can only strengthen the teamwork of parents and teachers in helping children develop to their greatest potential.

The resources are divided into those particularly relevant for staff—many of which relate to communicating and working with parents—and those for families. Resources in the latter group are often very useful for staff members as well; they are listed under Families because they are accessible presentations of introductory material on the topic at hand and/or because they include suggestions for what parents can do with children in a given area.

Staff

Barclay, K., and E. Boone. *Building a Three Way Partnership: The Leader's Role in Linking School, Family, and Community*. New York: Scholastic, 1995. ▶ Explores parent involvement, from written communication through school handbooks and newsletters to group meetings during open houses and parent programs to one-on-one meetings, and then expands school involvement to the local community.

Berger, E. *Parents as Partners in Education: The School and Home Working Together*. 3d. ed. New York: Merrill, 1991. ▶ A comprehensive look at parent involvement, providing a rationale for family involvement in early childhood programming, a historical overview of parent involvement, and specific suggestions for both school-based and home-based programs.

Burns, M. "Four Great Math Games," *Instructor* 103, no. 8 (1994): 44–45. ▶ Explains dice games that help children count and understand basic probability.

Chenfeld, M. *Teaching in the Key of Life*. Washington, DC: NAEYC, 1993. ▶ Reveals a teacher's passion for teaching in environments that lead children to the joy, curiosity, and discovery of learning—inspirational reading for teachers and parents alike.

Children's Software Revue, 44 Main St., Flemington, NJ 08822 (520 North Adams St.,Ypsilanti, MI 48197-2482); 908-284-0404, fax 908-284-0405. ▶ A newsletter providing timely reviews and information on latest resources; contains "All-Star Software" list of the magazine's top-rated programs.

Church, E. "How Many Ways Can You Move?" *Pre-K Today* 5, no. 5 (1991): 26–35. ▶ This perfect article for the beginning teacher gives very specific examples of activities to enhance movement in the classroom.

Croft, D. *Parents and Teachers: A Resource Book for Home, School, and Community Relations*. Albany, NY: Delmar, 1979. ▶ Offers practical suggestions on how to provide information about school to parents and how to share information about home with teachers.

Decker, L., G. Gregg, and V. Decker. *Getting Parents Involved in Their Children's Education*. Arlington, VA: American Association of School Administrators, 1994. ▶ Describes four models of parent involvement programs: protective, school-to-home transmission, curriculum enrichment, and partnership. Offers suggestions on starting a parent involvement program.

Dodge, D.T., and L. Colker. *The Creative Curriculum for Early Childhood*. 3d ed. Washington, DC: Teaching Strategies, 1988. ▶ Includes excellent sample letters to parents on what the program does in various areas of the curriculum and what parents can do.

Dombro, A. "Introducing Music," *Early Childhood Today* 9, no. 7 (1995): 46. ▶ Lists several influences of music on young children and gives many good reasons and tips for using music in early childhood classrooms.

Greenberg, P. "How and Why to Teach All Aspects of Preschool and Kindergarten Math Naturally, Democratically, and Effectively...Part 1," *Young Children* 48, no. 4 (1993): 75–84. ▶ Comparing a print-rich classroom to a "math-rich" classroom, Greenberg states that teachers need only apply the criteria for good teaching of young children to the teaching of mathematics. Lists appropriate math skills for preschool and kindergarten as well as good counting books.

Greenberg, P. "How and Why to Teach All Aspects of Preschool and Kindergarten Math, Part 2," *Young Children* 49, no. 2 (1994): 12–18. ▶ This follow-up article gives instruction to teachers about teaching sets in hands-on ways; includes helpful lists of books and resource materials, answers questions teachers often ask, and addresses gender equality in math instruction.

Haugland, S., and J. Wright. *Computers and Young Children: A World of Discovery*. New York: Allyn & Bacon, in press.

Honig, A. *Parent Involvement in Early Childhood Education*. Washington, DC: NAEYC, 1979. ▶ Discusses research on parent involvement programs that involve parents in early childhood programs.

Kristeller, J. "Creating Curriculum as a Workshop...An Interactive Process Involving Children, Teachers, and Families," *Early Childhood Today* 9, no. 3 (1994): 58–60. ▶Looks at the balance between planned and spontaneous elements in the early childhood curriculum. Chart presents criteria for selecting activities that support the growth and development of young children, and narratives guide the reader through actual events, problems, and solutions.

Neugebauer, B., ed. *Alike and Different: Exploring Our Humanity with Young Children.* Washington, DC: NAEYC, 1992. ▶The primary thesis of this book is that people with different abilities and experiences hold more in common than in conflict—most differences are interesting and enriching to the whole community, while others can be "mutually understood, negotiated, and lived with."

Ramsey, P., and L. Derman-Sparks. "Multicultural Education Reaffirmed," *Young Children* 47, no. 2 (1992): 10–11. ▶Challenges all early childhood educators to engage parents and community members in all attempts to implement antibias and multicultural curricula.

Riley, S. *How to Generate Values in Young Children: Integrity, Honesty, Individuality, Self-confidence, and Wisdom.* Washington, DC: NAEYC, 1984. ▶How we treat children makes a difference, whether the issue is toy selection, security blankets, toilet learning, or discipline. Parents love this book, too.

Schickedanz, J. *More Than the ABCs: The Early Stages of Reading and Writing.* Washington, DC: NAEYC, 1986. ▶Suggests ways in which parents, teachers, and caregivers can help children have meaningful reading and writing experiences.

Stone, J. *Teacher-Parent Relationships.* Brochure. Washington, DC: NAEYC, 1987. ▶Discusses the importance of relationships between parents and teachers during the early childhood years.

Swick, K. *Inviting Parents into the Young Child's World.* Champaign, IL: Stipes, 1984. ▶Acknowledges a child's need for continuity in his or her life; details how parents and teachers can work together to support young children; gives careful attention to the realities of today's busy and changing world.

Swick, K. *Teacher-Parent Partnerships to Enhance School Success in Early Childhood Education.* Washington, DC: National Education Association, 1991. ▶Defines the collaboration roles for both parents and teachers in developing partnerships; describes specific programs that have been found to be effective in developing and strengthening these partnerships.

Wright, J., and D. Shade. *Young Children: Active Learners in a Technological Age.* Washington, DC: NAEYC, 1994. ▶Argues that computers, when used properly, belong in early childhood programs—and explains how to integrate technology to benefit children's cognitive and social development.

Families

Ames, L. *Questions Parents Ask.* New York: Delta, 1988. ▶Answers questions about 31 different topics covering infants and preschoolers to preteens and teenagers.

Armstrong, T. *Seven Kinds of Smart.* New York: Penguin, 1993. ▶Simplifies psychologist Howard Gardner's work on the seven kinds of intelligences; helps parents determine which way their child learns best and suggests books, games, and software to encourage growth in each of the intelligences.

Balaban, N. *Learning to Say Good-bye: Starting School and Other Early Childhood Separations.* New York: Teachers College Press, 1985. ▶Offers practical suggestions to make separations smoother, from dealing with underlying feelings about separation to choosing a school that cares.

Cullinan, B. *Read to Me: Raising Kids Who Love to Read.* New York: Scholastic, 1992. ▶Stresses the connection between language and reading and shares ways for parents—even busy ones—to create reading times. An extended book list helps parents choose books for their children.

Curry, N., and C. Johnson. *Beyond Self-Esteem: Developing a Genuine Sense of Human Value.* Washington, DC: NAEYC, 1990. ▶Discusses how children develop self-esteem and meaningful ways that adults can promote true self-esteem in children.

Dinkmeyer, D., D. McKay, and J. Mckay. *New Beginnings: Skills for Single Parents and Stepfamily Parents.* Champaign, IL: Research Press, 1987. ▶Practical suggestions to help single parents and stepfamilies with issues such as new relationships, communication, decision-making, discipline, and parenting methods.

Dodge, D.T, and J. Phinney. *A Parent's Guide to Early Childhood Education.* Washington, DC: Teaching Strategies, 1990. ▶Clear, readable primer for communicating to parents the value of classroom activities of various kinds.

Dombro, A., and P. Bryan. *Sharing the Caring.* New York: Simon & Schuster, 1991. ▶Addresses both parents and providers on ways to build partnerships that will help children feel safe and secure in child care.

Elkind, D. *The Hurried Child: Growing Up Too Fast Too Soon.* Reading, MA: Addison-Wesley, 1988. ▶This classic confronts the reader with what families and society at large are doing to "make" children grow up too fast.

Essa, E., and C. Murray. "Young Children's Understanding and Experience with Death," *Young Children* 49, no. 4 (1994): 74–81. ▶Summarizes research about young children and their understanding about death, yet devotes two pages to practical suggestions for helping children cope with death.

Faber, A., and E. Mazlish. *How to Talk So Kids Will Listen and Listen So Kids Will Talk*. New York: Avon, 1982. ▶ Designed for workshop use with individual families or groups of families; topics include helping children deal with feelings, engaging cooperation, considering alternatives to punishment, encouraging autonomy, freeing children from playing roles. (A chairperson's guide and participant's workbook are available.)

Family PC, Box 400454, Des Moines, IA 50340-0454. ▶ Directed toward families with PCs, Macs, and multimedia but appropriate for educators, too.

Fenney, L. "Learning through Play: Music and Movement," *Pre-K Today* 6, no. 2 (1991): 20.   This page is reproducible for parents, offering hints on incorporating musical enjoyment into their everyday activities with their children.

Fraiberg, S. *The Magic Years: Understanding and Handling Problems of Early Childhood*. New York: Scribners, 1984. ▶ Concentrating on infancy through age 6, this classic discusses emotional issues that arise during this critical period in the lives of young children.

Frede, E. *Getting Involved: Workshops for Parents*. Ypsilanti, MI: High/Scope Press, 1984. ▶ Suggests a variety of workshops for parents, including attitudes toward learning, play, language, reading, writing, math, science, television, and problem solving.

Galvin, E. "The Joy of Seasons: With the Children, Discover the Joys of Nature," *Young Children* 49, no. 4 (1994): 4–9. ▶ Follows the four seasons and gives specific examples of nature studies for young children; emphasizes that adults do not have to be able to identify all items in nature for these studies to be beneficial.

Goldhaber, J. "Sticky to Dry, Red to Purple: Exploring Transformation with Playdough," *Young Children* 48, no. 1 (1992): 26–28. ▶ Discusses what children do with and learn from playdough if they are allowed extended opportunities to interact with the simple material.

Green, E. *Read Me a Story: Books and Techniques for Reading Aloud and Storytelling*. Garden City, NY: Preschool, 1992. ▶ This easy-to-read, pamphlet-like book presents information on the importance of sharing stories with children, how to choose stories, and techniques for reading aloud.

Greenberg, P. *Character Development: Encouraging Self-Esteem and Self-Discipline in Infants, Toddlers, and Two-Year-Olds*. Washington, DC: NAEYC, 1991. ▶ Twelve thoughtful essays, with practical, problem-solving points of view, that provide the basics for developing good people as we work with young children.

Healy, J. *Endangered Minds*. New York: Touchstone, 1990. ▶ Examines the reasons children today are less able to concentrate, less able to absorb and analyze information; argues that the basic intelligence of children has not changed—society has.

Healy, J. *Your Child's Grown Mind*. New York: Doubleday, 1987. ▶ Explains how a child's mind develops, dispels the "superbaby" myth, and points out the damage that can be done when parents pressure young children to read before they are developmentally ready.

Honig, A. *Love and Learn: Discipline for Young Children*. Brochure. Washington, DC: NAEYC, 1985. ▶ Positive approaches that work.

Jalongo, M. "Helping Children to Cope with Relocation," *Childhood Education* 71, no. 2 (1995): 80–85. ▶ Describes parents and teacher strategies for preparing children to relocate and helping them to adjust to the new environment; vignettes illustrate the effects of moving on young children.

Jalongo, M. *Young Children and Picture Books: Literature from Infancy to Six*. Washington, DC: NAEYC, 1988. ▶ Supplies rationale for learning to read through meaningful experiences and daily exposure to books; includes an outstanding, concise resource for selecting and connecting the best picture books and young children.

Kutner, L. "I Hate You!" *Parents Magazine* 67, no. 12 (1992): 192–93. ▶ Argues that when young children sometimes claim to hate their parents, this is a normal way children express anger.

McCabe, A. *Language Games to Play with Your Child*. New York: Insight, 1992. ▶ Provides descriptions of children's language development from infancy to adolescence and suggests games and other activities to support oral and, later, written language.

McCormick, P. 1994. "'It's mine!' Learning to Share Doesn't Come Naturally," *Parents Magazine* 69, no. 4 (1994): 86–90. ▶ Shares ways to help children learn the value of sharing with other children.

McCracken, J. *Play Is FUNdamental*. Brochure (also available in Spanish version, *El juego es fundamanetal*). Washington, DC: NAEYC, 1987. ▶ Explains how play helps children learn in all sorts of ways and how parents and teachers can make play an enriching experience.

McCracken, J. *Reducing Stress in Young Children's Lives*. Washington, DC: NAEYC, 1986. ▶ This collection of articles previously published in the journal *Young Children* offers practical advice on how to help children cope with everyday stresses and the more intense stresses related to divorce, death, or abuse.

Mitchell, G. *Common Sense Discipline*. Glen Burnie, MD: Telshare, 1995. ▶Gives practical ideas and suggestions for all adults who work with young children.

Mitchell, G. *A Very Practical Guide to Discipline with Young Children*. New York: Telshare, 1982. ▶This easy-to-read book helps parents apply gentle forms of discipline to handle many typical problems, such as getting children to bed and biting.

Myhre, S. "Enhancing Your Dramatic-Play Area through the Use of Prop Boxes," *Young Children* 48, no. 5 (1993): 6–11. ▶Filled with suggestions for creating and using prop boxes to spur dramatic play themes for young children.

National Association for the Education of Young Children. *Helping Children Learn Self-Control: A Guide to Discipline*. Brochure. Washington, DC: Author, 1986. ▶Basic techniques to help children develop self-discipline.

Peterson, R., and V. Felton-Collins. *The Piaget Handbook for Teachers and Parents: Children in the Age of Discovery, Preschool–Third Grade*. New York: Teachers College Press, 1986. ▶An excellent, easy reader for those interested in understanding Piaget's theory of cognitive development in young children; topics include the importance of play, language development, learning through questioning, math experience, and implications drawn from Piaget's work for teachers and parents.

Poest, C. "Challenge Me to Move: Large Muscle Development in Young Children," *Young Children* 45, no. 5 (1990): 4–10. ▶Reinforces the importance of large motor skill development in young children and offers teachers activities to enhance these skills.

Rich, D. *Megaskills*. New York: Houghton Mifflin, 1992. ▶Translates research about the importance of families' influence on children into practical, specific activities that teach values such as confidence, motivation, effort, responsibility, initiative, perseverance, caring, teamwork, common sense, and problem solving.

Riley, S. *How to Generate Values in Young Children*. Washington, DC: NAEYC, 1984. ▶Discusses the complexities of life that inhibit the development of values in young children and offers practical suggestions about how adults can counter these influences.

Samalin, N. *Loving Your Child Is Not Enough*. New York: Penguin, 1987. ▶Offers suggestions for avoiding daily battles, providing constructive criticism, coping with sibling dilemmas, and working with our own anger and self-esteem issues.

Sawyers, J., and C. Rogers. *Helping Young Children Develop Through Play: A Practical Guide for Parents, Caregivers, and Teachers*. Washington, DC: NAEYC, 1988. ▶Reminds parents and teachers of the importance of play for young children; offers practical suggestions for supporting the play of babies, toddlers, preschoolers, and primary-age children.

Shirk, M. "Family Travel," *Parents Magazine* 67, no. 4 (1992): 141–62. ▶Suggests great places for family vacations; gives health and safety tips, travel notes, and other ideas for surviving life on the road.

Taylor, D., and D. Strickland. *Family Storybook Reading*. Portsmouth, NH: Heinemann, 1986. ▶Informative book focusing on the importance of storybook reading in family life and in acquiring literacy skills.

Trelease, J. *The New Read Aloud Handbook*. New York: Penguin Books, 1989. ▶No library should be without this valuable explanation of why, when, where, and how to read to young children.

Townsend-Butterworth, D. *Your Child's First School: A Handbook for Parents*. New York: Walker & Company, 1992. ▶Acknowledges the many decisions parents have to make about their child's education; provides detailed information about early childhood programs and elementary school options; gives practical advice about how to prepare kids for group educational experiences.

Weissbord, B. "Mommy, Please Don't Go!" *Parents Magazine* 67, no.1 (1992): 230. ▶Offers practical solutions for dealing with separation anxiety; discusses consequences of separation at a young age and explains how to handle setbacks.

Williams, R., R. Rockwell, and E. Sherwood. *Mudpies to Magnets*. Mt. Ranier, MD: Gryphon House, 1987. ▶Here are 112 ready-to-use science experiments that provide hands-on learning.

Further Resources from NAEYC

Bjorklund, G., and C. Burger. "Making Conferences Work for Parents, Teachers, and Children," *Young Children* 42, no. 2 (1987): 26–31.

Boutte, G., D. Keepler, V. Tyler, and B. Terry. "Effective Techniques for Involving 'Difficult' Parents," *Young Children* 47, no. 3 (1992): 18–22.

Bredekamp, S., and C. Copple, eds. 1997. *Developmentally appropriate practice in early childhood programs*. Rev. ed. Washington, DC: NAEYC.

Brock, D., and E. Dodd. "A Family Lending Library: Promoting Early Literacy Development," *Young Children* 49, no. 3 (1994): 16–17.

Bundy, B. "Fostering Communication between Parents and Preschools," *Young Children* 46, no. 2 (1991): 12–17.

Coleman, M. "Planning for the Changing Nature of Family Life in Schools for Young Children," *Young Children* 46, no. 4 (1991): 15–20.

Diffily, D. "The Project Approach: A Museum Exhibit Created by Kindergartners," *Young Children* 51, no. 2 (1996): 72-75.

Dimidjian, V. "Holidays, Holy Days, and Wholly Dazed: Approaches to Special Days," *Young Children* 44, no. 6 (1989): 70–75.

Edson, A. "Crossing the Great Divide: The Nursery School Child Goes to Kindergarten," *Young Children* 49, no. 5 (1994): 69–75.

Foster, S. "Successful Parent Meetings," *Young Children* 50, no. 1 (1994): 78-81.

Gottschall, S., "Understanding and Accepting Separation Feelings," *Young Children* 44, no. 6 (1989): 11–16.

Greenwood, D. "Home-School Communication via Video," *Young Children* 50, no. 6 (1995): 66.

Harding, N. "Family Journals: The Bridge from School to Home and Back Again," *Young Children* 51, no. 2 (1996): 25–30.

Haugland, S., and D. Shade. "Developmentally Appropriate Software for Young Children," *Young Children* 43, no. 4 (1988): 37–43.

Helm, J. "Family Theme Bags: An Innovative Approach to Family Involvement in the School," *Young Children* 49, no. 4 (1994): 48–52

Kantrowitz, B., and P. Wingert. "How Kids Learn," *Young Children* 44, no. 6 (1989): 3–10. Reprinted from *Newsweek*, 17 April 1989.

Kelman, A. "Choices for Children," *Young Children* 45, no. 3 (1990): 42–45.

Kokoski, T., and N. Downing-Leffler. "Boosting Your Science and Home-school Connection," *Young Children* 50, no. 5 (1995): 35–39.

Krogh, S., and L. Lamme. "But What about Sharing? Children's Literature and Moral Development," *Young Children* 40, no. 4 (1985): 48–51.

Levin, D., and N. Carlsson-Paige. "Developmentally Appropriate Television: Putting Children First," *Young Children* 49, no. 5 (1994): 38–44.

Manning, M., G. Manning, and G. Morrison. "Letter-Writing Connections: A Teacher, First-Graders, and Their Parents," *Young Children* 50, no. 6 (1995): 34–38.

Mavrogenes, N. "Helping Parents Help Their Children Become Literate," *Young Children* 45, no. 4 (1990): 4–9.

McBride, B. "Interaction, Accessibility, and Responsibility: A View of Father Involvement and How to Encourage It," *Young Children* 44, no. 5 (1989): 13–19.

Morgan, E. "Talking with Parents when Concerns Come Up," *Young Children* 44, no. 2 (1989): 52–56.

Poest, C., J. Williams, D. Witt, and M. Atwood. "Challenge Me to Move: Large Muscle Development in Young Children," *Young Children* 45, no. 5 (1990): 4–10.

Rivkin, M., ed. "Science Is a Way of Life," *Young Children* 47, no. 4 (1992): 4–8.

Spewock, T. "Teaching Parents of Young Children through Learning Packets," *Young Children* 47, no. 1 (1991): 28–30.

Spiegel, D., J. Fitzgerald, and J. Cunningham. "Parental Perceptions of Preschoolers' Literacy Development: Implications for Home-School Partnerships," *Young Children* 48, no. 5 (1993): 74–79.

Stipek, D., L. Rosenblatt, and L. DiRocco. "Making Parents Your Allies," *Young Children* 49, no. 3 (1994): 4–9.

Various authors. "Viewpoints on Violence" (1—Video Game Violence, B. Klemm; 2—Is Gun Play OK Here? J. Kuykendall; 3—Making Friends with the Power Rangers, J. Greenberg; 4—Can Teachers Resolve the War-Play Dilemma? N. Carlsson-Paige and D. Levin), *Young Children* 50, no. 5 (1995): 52–63.

Information about NAEYC

NAEYC is . . .

. . . a membership-supported organization of people committed to fostering the growth and development of children from birth through age 8. Membership is open to all who share a desire to serve and act on behalf of the needs and rights of young children.

NAEYC provides . . .

. . . educational services and resources to adults who work with and for children, including

- *Young Children,* the journal for early childhood educators
- **books, posters, brochures,** and **videos** to expand your knowledge and commitment to young children, with topics including infants, curriculum, research, discipline, teacher education, and parent involvement
- an **Annual Conference** that brings people together from all over the country to share their expertise and advocate on behalf of children and families
- **Week of the Young Child** celebrations sponsored by NAEYC Affiliate Groups across the nation to call public attention to the needs and rights of children and families
- **insurance plans** for individuals and programs
- **public affairs** information and access to information available through NAEYC resources and communication systems for knowledgeable advocacy efforts at all levels of government and through the media
- the **National Academy of Early Childhood Programs,** a voluntary accreditation system for high-quality programs for children
- the **National Institute for Early Childhood Professional Development,** which offers resources and services to improve professional preparation and development of early childhood educators
- **Young Children International** to promote international communication and information exchanges

For free information about membership, publications, or other NAEYC services, visit the **NAEYC Website** at **http://www.naeyc.org/naeyc**

National Association for the Education of Young Children
1509 16th Street, NW
Washington, DC 20036-1426
202-232-8777 or 800-424-2460